SUREFIRE

WITHDRAWN

55 Surefire
HOMEBASED BUSINESSES
You Can Start for *Under $5,000*

Photographer • Gift Basket Design • Cleaning Service • Consultant • Event Planner • Herbal/Farm-Related • Home Inspector • Personal Concierge • Mail Order • Pet Sitter • Editorial Service • Wedding Consultant • Financial Planner • Accountant • Tax Preparer • Bed & Breakfast • Bookkeeper • Taxidermist • eBay Assistant • Notary Public • Real Estate Property Management • Justice of the Peace • Website Developer • Freelance Designer • Dog Breeder/Kennel • Flea Market • Daycare • Christmas Tree Farm • Appliance Repair • Chimney Sweep • Computer Repair • and Many More

s & Cheryl Kimball

Jere L. Calmes, Publisher
Cover Design: Beth Hansen-Winter
Composition and Production: MillerWorks

This publication is designed to provide accurate and authoritative information in regard to the subject matter covered. It is sold with the understanding that the publisher is not engaged in rendering legal, accounting or other professional services. If legal advice or other expert assistance is required, the services of a competent professional person should be sought.

Library of Congress Cataloging-in-Publication Data

Kimball, Cheryl.
55 surefire homebased businesses you can start for under $5,000 / by Entrepreneur Press and Cheryl Kimball.
    p. cm. — (Surefire series)
  ISBN 978-1-59918-256-8 (alk. paper)
  1. Home-based businesses. 2. New business enterprises Management.
  I. Title. II. Title: Fifty-five surefire homebased businesses you can start for under $5,000.
HD62.38.K537 2008   658.1'1412—dc22
2008020618

Printed in Canada

12 11 10 09   10 9 8 7 6 5 4 3 2 1

CONTENTS

THE FUNDAMENTALS OF HAVING A HOMEBASED BUSINESS

Today, tens of thousands of people are considering starting a homebased business, and for good reasons. On average, people can expect to have two and three careers during their work life. Those leaving one career often think about their second or third career move being to their own home. People who have been part of the traditional nine-to-five work force and are on the verge of retiring from that life are thinking of what to do next. The good news: Starting a homebased business is within the reach of almost anyone who wants to take a risk and work hard.

This book tells you about some of the most commonly successful homebased businesses that don't take a lot of capital to start. It includes a few that aren't so common, but also have success written all over them.

But before you get too excited, there are many things to mull over before deciding to combine your home and your workplace.

THINGS TO CONSIDER

Other Household Members

The first thing to consider before you set up shop at home is the feelings of the people with whom you live. How will your business idea impact their day-to-day life? How will your being at home a lot of the time change the household dynamic? Will the space you need for your business interfere with daily activities at home?

This is when you need to sit down and have that family meeting, Brady Bunch style. Lay your plans out on the table. Find out what the others think; this is a big deal for the family, and most people feel better about changes if they are consulted first.

If you have a spouse and two more young children, the impact is going to be greater than if it is just you. But many people choose to start a homebased business when they have young children because working at home allows you to work around the kids' schedules, making sure someone is always home when they are.

Other people wait until children are more self-sufficient or on their way to college before setting up shop at home—that empty bedroom looks like an appealing place for a home office!

Whomever is in the household—spouse, children, parents—be sure to consult them before making your final decision.

Space

A next big consideration is space. Do you have the space at home to do the work you are thinking about doing? Will you need a separate room, or will a corner of the living room or that alcove off the kitchen be enough? Do you need storage space? Is there room in the garage or a shed that you could use for storage? Will you need an office with a separate client entrance or will you go to them almost 100 percent of the time?

Because we will be discussing businesses you can start for under $5,000, building an addition onto your house or renovating half the garage into a workspace does not make fiscal sense when you are starting up. Many homebased businesses need nothing more than an office space that can accommodate a computer workstation. Keep in mind that if you plan to take a tax deduction for your home office, your workspace cannot be used for anything but your business.

Insurance

You need to check your homeowner's insurance policy to determine if the business you are planning to start is covered under your policy. Check that your business equipment replacement costs are covered. If your business requires that clients come to your home office, check that this is covered under your homeowner's insurance plan. You may find you need separate riders for some specifics about your business that your homeowner's policy does not cover.

Zoning

One of the most common mistakes people make is assuming that because their neighbor has a homebased business, the zoning must be OK for any homebased business. This is far from the truth.

First, your neighbor's business may not be legal under the zoning guidelines. Just because someone has a business in their home doesn't mean they are following the rules. Second, your business may fall under a different set of rules than your neighbor's business. And finally, lots of people are surprised to learn that zoning can be different at one end of a road than the other.

But don't get too alarmed; you probably don't need to be in a commercial zone to have your business. Most towns have zoning laws that accommodate low-impact home businesses. If your business doesn't generate significant traffic to your small residential neighborhood or if there aren't environmental considerations, even neighborhoods that are zoned residential often allow homebased businesses. Other zoning regulations include signage, driveway requirements, and considerations specific to your town. You need to research and follow local regulations for every aspect of your business.

The bottom line is that it is important to check the zoning laws for your specific location. You don't want to go to the trouble of starting your business to find out it is illegal to have it in your home.

Mileage

Several of the businesses listed in this book require some kind of transportation to get you from your home to the client. This can be your personal vehicle—you won't be able to buy a specific business vehicle and keep your startup costs under $5,000!

Using your personal vehicle is fine. However, to keep the IRS happy, be sure to keep a travel log of all the mileage you put on your personal vehicle for your business. You will want to record the date, the starting mileage, the ending mileage, where you went, and why you went there. When tax time comes around, you'll add up the miles and use that total to compute the expense you can to write off as business mileage.

If you need a vehicle for a more substantial business use than just getting from here to there—such as a van with storage space or a pickup truck for hauling—you should consider leasing. Your lease payments are tax deductible if your leased vehicle is used strictly for business. Because you can often get a lease with a very low down payment, you won't need to trade in your personal vehicle, and keep business and personal travel completely separate.

HOW THIS BOOK IS ORGANIZED

In the following pages, you will find 55 homebased businesses to consider. Each business idea starts with some opening information, including a little about the business idea in general, what kind of special training or experience you might need to be successful, and several ways you can specialize in that particular business category. Under each listing you will also find discussions on the following categories.

How This Business Impacts Your Home

This section talks about what kind of impact this type of business may have on day-to-day life at your home. Will you need to have an office where the door locks to keep your client's tax records safe? Is it important for the type of business you are opening that clients come to your office and that they arrive to a beautifully landscaped yard? This section helps you think through the reality of your home with its new business in it.

Things to Consider

This section is intended to point out things about each business that you need to keep in mind, such as: you will need lots of inventory storage space, or this business is physically demanding, or to succeed you will need to have worked in the industry and have lots of potential clients, etc.

How Do You Want to Spend Your Day?

What do you consider to be the perfect work day? One where you are done with work by noon? One where you are on your feet most of the time or one that you are sitting at a desk most of the time? One where you can lock yourself in your office and be alone doing research or one where you are interacting with people most of the day?

The great thing about most homebased businesses is that even if your business requires you to be sitting in front of a computer a lot, when you work for yourself at home, you are pretty much free to get up and take the dog for a brisk walk around the neighborhood or sit with the kids and share an afternoon snack or stretch your legs and clear your head any time you need to.

But it pays in the long run to be clear about what you imagine your best day to be and find a business that fits that picture as closely as possible.

What You Need

Almost all businesses require a computer workstation, even if it is just to keep your records and bookkeeping up to date. But many businesses have special requirements. Those will be listed here, including any special vehicle or storage needs.

Marketing Angle

Every business has its own marketing approach. This short section gives you an idea of what marketing you will have to do in order to get your business up and running and keep it successful.

Nice Touch

This section gives you some ideas on how you can go the extra mile with your customers to give them a lasting and positive impression of you, your business, and your services. Whether it's a frequent-buyer program or a vase of fresh flowers left on the counter each time you clean a household, these are the kinds of things that will have customers telling their friends and family about your business.

Expansion Possibilities

Many businesses start out modestly and expand into other areas in order to grow the business. This section provides a few ideas of where you might be able to go in the future if you started this type of business.

Words to Know

As you learn about a business idea, there are some words you need to know to understand the business. The mini glossary with each business points out three or four fundamental terms you will run across as you explore the idea further. The glossary is by no means extensive, but just a taste of some of the terminology.

Resources

Each business idea is accompanied by several resources, such as trade magazines and websites. These are not intended as endorsements of these companies or products, but rather, they offer an opportunity for you to get a further sense of what you might be getting yourself into!

IN GENERAL

No matter what homebased business you start, there are some general things common to all businesses, and a few things taken for granted to keep your start-up homebased business within the "under $5,000" criteria.

Vehicles

This is probably the biggest concern when keeping your business under $5,000. If a business requires a van or truck to haul equipment, it would be difficult to find an appropriate vehicle of that nature for under $5,000. Even if the purchase price meets that criteria, you might have to put additional money into it to make it roadworthy and suitable for your business.

The assumption here is that you will either already own the appropriate vehicle or you will lease it. Leasing often requires very little down payment, if any, and the monthly lease payment generally can be written off on your taxes as a business expense (but be sure to check with your tax accountant on any tax information).

There are a couple of advantages to leasing: It offers you a way into the business without investing in purchasing an expensive vehicle, and you can trade the vehicle in at the end of the lease and either buy at that time or lease a new vehicle.

There are also a couple disadvantages to keep in mind. By leasing, you have no equity in the vehicle. In addition, if you decide to get out of your business before the end of the lease period, you may pay a penalty for returning the vehicle before the lease is out. Check the fine print on this or whether you can sublease the vehicle for the remainder of the lease period.

Business Cards

Always carry business cards with you. If you have a computer (see "Basic Computer Workstation" later in this section), you can create business cards easily and inexpensively. Many word processing programs include templates that you can customize by plugging in your business information, and you can print your cards on perforated business card stock carried by most office supply stores.

Include your business name, your name, the business address, phone number, fax number, e-mail address, and website address on the business card. If your business name is self-explanatory or if there is room for a short sell line on the card—"Childcare in a Home Setting" or "Pet-sitting by a Certified Vet Tech"—your card can double as an ad posted on community bulletin boards.

Advertising

You'll need to advertise your new business. Advertising doesn't have to be extensive or complicated, but if you are serious about your business, you need to have your name out there and you'll need to anticipate advertising expenses in your start-up capital. Place a small display ad in the weekly free newspaper and keep it going, because multiple advertising insertions of your ad will have the greatest impact. Readers of the paper may not need pet-sitting or home inspection services right now, but when they do, they will remember that they've seen your ad in the paper or on the menu of the diner they visit regularly.

Create a Website

These days, almost everyone goes the to internet for information about a service or product. Be sure that they find you when they are searching for what you have to offer. Creating a simple website couldn't be easier. Register a domain name through one of the popular sites such as GoDaddy.com. Use it to create a basic website. Many internet service providers offer free website templates. Pay the small monthly fee to a hosting service to keep it up and running. Add a blog to give website visitors added value. Learn a little bit about search engine optimization so that when surfers search using words that relate to your business, your website appears on the first or second page of matches.

Start simple; you can build and change your website as you go along to keep it interesting and up to date. At the very least, provide visitors with the basic information they need to get in touch with you.

A Business Is a Business

Even though you are homebased and starting your business on a shoestring, always treat your business like a business. Expect to get adequately and fairly compensated for the work you do. Be careful to charge for all supplies. Get the appropriate insurance coverage to protect your assets. And act professionally at all times.

Write a Business Plan

A key part of establishing a serious business is to create a business plan. This multi-section document can be simply for your own purposes to help you to better understand and organize your business, to plan expansion, or to present to a financial institution or investors to gain start-up or expansion funding. A business plan consists of:

- an overview of your business
- market research of the general business climate in this industry in your area, including any competing businesses

- a marketing plan that shows how you are going to advertise and promote your business to bring in customers

- background information about you, your resume, and similar information about any key employees or partners

- financial statements, including a personal income statement, projected start-up expenses, and pro forma profit and loss statements month-by-month for one year

- any sample contracts or other legal documents relating to the business, such as equipment leasing contracts

If you take the time to do a thorough business plan, you may be surprised by the number of times you refer to this document in your first year of business.

Basic Computer Workstation

Almost any business you decide to undertake will require a basic computer and peripherals. You should plan to have the following:

- **A desktop computer.** A PC equipped with the latest Pentium processor, 320-500GB of hard drive memory, 2-3GB of RAM (short-term memory), and the ability to burn DVDs and CDs, will cost approximately $500.

- **Large-screen monitor, 17-19."** You can get a TV-like flat-panel monitor for approximately $200. Look for high resolution (1440 x 900) and good contrast (500:1).

- **Accessories.** You will need a keyboard and a mouse to get going. If your chosen business requires working on the computer a lot, you may want to consider an ergonomic keyboard—once you get used to it, you will never go back. Most any mouse will do; pick the one that feels best in your hand. You can also choose to go wireless on both of these accessories and keep your desk a little more clutter-free.

- **Connections.** Check that your computer comes with all the power cords and cables you need to get up and running.

- **The whole works.** A PC desktop package with everything included in the box (computer, monitor, keyboard, and mouse) will total about $1,000. An Apple iMac, which is an all-in-one Macintosh system, with a 20-inch monitor, mouse, and keyboard, will cost approximately $1200. Often packages are bundled with an inkjet printer, so shop around.

- **Internet service.** Sign up with an internet service provider (ISP). If dial-up is all that is available in your area at the moment, so be it. Otherwise, go straight to high-speed internet access via your phone service or a cable provider like TimeWarner or Comcast. The difference is worth every penny.

- **Internet connections.** You will need a modem (usually provided by the ISP) and a cable long enough to reach from the modem to your computer. If you choose to use a laptop computer as your main computer, and your laptop has a wireless card, you may want to add wireless internet access to your home. You will need to purchase a router to receive the wireless connection and send it around your immediate area. You may also need a booster, if the area in which you wish to have internet access is large or has many obstructions. But if being able to move around your house with your laptop is important, or if you'd like access to your e-mail and do online research while you have lunch in a wi-fi café, in then by all means consider wireless internet.

You will also need some other computer-run machines, known as peripherals. These might include:

- **Printer.** A printer is a must. Printers have gone up in quality and down in price. If you will mostly be using your printer to print out invoices and statements, you can get away with the most basic of printers with a price tag of under $200. If your business calls for printing out product information sheets, photos of any kind, or other printed material to be given to customers, consider a higher quality printer. You can choose between inkjet and laser, both of which run anywhere from $150-$500.

- **Scanner.** A scanner allows you to scan photos and text and save them in digitized form. Scanners are so inexpensive (under $200) that for the couple times you might use one, they can be worth having around.

- **Fax machine.** Though not technically a computer peripheral, you should definitely pick up a fax machine. A standalone fax machine generally costs under $100.

- **All-in-One.** These office multi-taskers are scanner, printer, and fax machine combined, and have the ability to print photos directly from your digital camera or the camera's memory card as well. These are pretty handy and they do make sense considering all of these functions operate in pretty much the same way. However, if something fundamental breaks down on the machine or one component needs to be repaired, you are without all of these functions! For some businesses, that may not be a big issue and these all-in-one machines are excellent choices. For others, it is not the best choice and getting separate machines for each function is the better route.

- **Camera.** Any business can benefit from having a digital camera. You can use it to take product shots to put on your own website or on eBay. You can take photos of your finished jobs to put them on your website or add them to marketing materials. Prices for high-quality digital cameras have come down in recent years, and you can now get an excellent all-purpose camera for under $600.

HAPPY HUNTING

So that is the basics of what you need to get started, and now you are ready to pick your homebased business. There are 55 great ideas here, a few of which surely have your name on them!

ICON KEY

 $ = $1500 or less to startup

 $$ = $1500-3000 to startup

 $$$ = $3000-5000 to startup

 = Some experience, special training, and/or licensing may be needed

 = Has great expansion possibilities

PHOTOGRAPHER

Have you always enjoyed taking pictures? Are you the family historian, snapping away at holiday gatherings? Then photography might be a great homebased business for you.

Making money as a photographer can be done in a number of different ways. You can specialize in one area, the most common being weddings. Another way to specialize as a photographer is to take pictures at events like antique car shows or horse shows or corporate events.

There are other niches you can explore for photography: portraits of people and their pets, families, and homes; photographs of holiday events, birthday parties or Christmas cards; the possibilities are endless.

Think about your own hobbies and interests. Your photography services to, for example, the antique car show market will be much more marketable if you know the subject matter. As an antique car aficionado yourself, you would know what kinds of shots people would like of their cars, what pieces of a particular antique car are especially unique or photogenic, and what kinds of view shows the car off best.

If you decide to go the niche route, you will need to take some free photos for a while to be able to showcase your talent. In a photography business, pictures are definitely worth a thousand words.

If you just like wandering around taking interesting photos of landscapes and scenes, there are several online stock photo companies that buy photos. Some will pay outright for the highest quality photos, others basically work on consignment—you post your photos on their site and once a month you get a check for the number of photos, and number of times each photo gets downloaded by someone.

Once you decide what kind of photography you would like to specialize in, you need to get a camera! Unless you want to specialize in large format or other traditional types of photography, digital is the way to go. Any good photographer will only get one shot out of twenty that are worth printing. By using digital cameras, you no longer have to process (and pay for) hundreds of slides or prints to find that one useable shot, or look at endless proof sheets to decide which photos might be worth having printed. Working digitally, you can snap away, with your only recurring cost being the memory cards used in your camera.

Besides a camera, you'll need to have a good computer on which to view your shots. You'll need a good monitor for accurate viewing of your photos, and the right software to allow you to easily view and manipulate your images. Your computer needs to be fast and have lots of RAM since high-resolution color photos tend to be very large files.

Many professional photographers create digital portfolios, allowing clients to view their work online at their leisure, and then order prints. This is helpful for a home-based operation; it's not necessary for clients to come to your home to view and pick their shots.

HOW THIS BUSINESS WILL IMPACT YOUR HOME

Depending on what kind of photography you decide to do, you may want a designated studio space in your home. If you do portrait photography, you will need to find out zoning laws in your area concerning having a business with foot traffic. And you need to check out your homeowner's insurance and add a rider or a separate policy covering liability issues for potential incidents with clients (tripping on the stairs, slipping on an icy sidewalk). Generally what you will need for your home is a place to set up a computer with a wide screen and an ergonomically comfortable workstation; you may think you will be out taking photos most of the time, but you will find yourself spending a lot of time at the computer manipulating those digital images.

THINGS TO CONSIDER

A professional photography career no longer means spending hours and hours in a darkroom working with toxic chemicals. However, that part of photography has been replaced with spending lots of time working with computers and software. If you are "computer-phobic," this can be a problem. You need to be able to install software, learn new programs, and understand your computer system in order to be efficient.

HOW DO YOU WANT TO SPEND YOUR DAY?

Being a wedding photographer means almost exclusively weekend work—and that means every weekend during the peak wedding season of June through September. If you have a spouse or partner who works a nine-to-five job all week, starting a business where you will be gone evenings and weekends may put a strain on your relationship.

WHAT YOU WILL NEED

- **Digital camera.** You'll want to have two to three different lenses, a case, and a couple memory cards.

- **Computer.** Make sure it is loaded with lots of RAM and has a generous amount of storage on the hard drive.

- **Monitor and printer.** A laptop is useful to be able to download the camera on site, but laptops are more expensive than desktop computers. You probably won't want to purchase two computers, so if you do go for a laptop, buy a large-screen monitor to use at home.

- **Website.**

- **CDs and DVDs.** Burn each job on its own CD or DVD. A backup hard drive is also recommended.

- **Transportation.** Depending on the type of photography you choose to specialize in, you will most likely need a vehicle, but your personal automobile is sufficient. See the introduction for information on keeping travel records.

MARKETING ANGLE

The marketing angle you take for your photography business will depend on what focus (pardon the pun) you've chosen for your business. If you decide to go the wedding photography route, this is a very easy market to get to—there are wedding shows, wedding-specific shops and websites, wedding magazines, wedding services, etc. Anyone planning a wedding is checking into any or all of these wedding-related outlets. Of course, the fact that there is such a targeted market also means there will be LOTS of competition! This is where your advertising and marketing plan comes into play.

For other types of photography, you will also need to direct your advertising and marketing toward magazines, newsletters, online sites through website link exchanges, and any other way you can think of. For instance, if you want to do antique car photography, plan to spend lots of weekends hanging out at antique car shows. Take photos, buy a booth at the exhibit, pay to hang a banner with your website address—anything to draw your target audience in to take a look at your photos.

NICE TOUCH

Purchase a portable photo printer you can bring with you and leave a sample prints behind for your client so they can have an idea of how the shots will come out.

EXPANSION POSSIBILITIES

Expansion in the photography business means using your photos for multiple purposes—i.e., getting paid more than once for a photo. If you retain rights to your photos, selling them with nonexclusive use as often as possible, you can sell the use of same photo many times; for instance, for use in a calendar, as a greeting card, in a book, on a book cover, in a brochure, etc. You can also post your photo on a stock photo company website such as Shutterstock, and get paid a royalty for each time someone downloads your photo from the site.

Another way to expand your business would be to hire people who can do the production work for you while you are out doing the actual photography. But ultimately, there is only one you and only so much time in a day—you need to hone your skills, make a name for yourself, get lots of work, and be able to charge top prices for your photography.

WORDS TO KNOW

Megapixels: Millions of pixels. The pixel count (usually indicated in megapixels) is one of several factors that determine the quality of the image a digital camera will provide. More pixels means more information is gathered by the camera, resulting in a higher resolution file, and a higher quality image.

Memory card: A common storage system for digital cameras; these cards can often be put right into a computer or printer for easy downloads.

SLR (Single Lens Reflex): A type of camera that uses a mirror system to direct light from the lens through the viewfinder eyepiece, allowing the photographer to see exactly what is being captured through the lens by the camera. This is the format of traditional 35mm cameras, but SLRs are now available in digital format as well.

Resources

Photographycorner.com

Photographytips.com

Professionalphotographysupply.com

GIFT BASKET SERVICE

2

If you have a craftsy touch, consider starting a gift basket business. Baskets will always put a smile on someone's face and can be a rewarding business venture.

Everyone from parents to friends to corporations is a potential customer for sending a gift basket. Baskets are common as new baby gifts, birthday gifts, and holidays. Of course, the Easter basket is *the* quintessential basket!

Because gift baskets can hold just about anything, finding a niche is the best way to start out in the gift basket business. Do you have a particular interest or special expertise that could lend itself to gift basket creations? Are you a dog lover, horse lover, or exercise guru who could put together baskets that hold the things that people with this interest would like?

Do you already create a product that a gift basket could be built around? Have you made your own soaps for the past ten years? For example, a gift basket that included one or two of your soaps, hand lotion, a scrub brush, and manicure kit could be a lovely basket to receive. Or if you are into making candles, you could build a basket that includes some of your special handmade candles, candle holders, a candle snuffer, and even wine glasses to round out a candlelit dinner.

A great way to focus your gift basket business is to concentrate on corporate accounts. Many corporations send gift baskets to the hotel rooms of visiting clients. Perhaps the corporation makes a product that the basket could be built around. Corporate accounts mean more money with fewer clients, which can really streamline your business. In order to get these accounts, you want to have a few baskets designed to show the purchaser to prove that you can create a quality product that will best represent their company.

Some corporations even hold regular conferences where you could get an order for over a hundred of the same basket. This is the kind of customer you can build your gift basket business around!

Great fun can be had purchasing items to put into gift baskets. But be sure to not go wild pre-purchasing inventory. If you want to specialize in a certain type of basket, you can be more confident that larger quantities of a product will be sold. But if you plan to customize according to the needs and wants of each customer who comes along, you don't want a huge supply of widget that will end up in only two customers' baskets— even if the widgets were a great price per thousand. The price tends to become less great when you use only five of those thousand widgets.

HOW THIS BUSINESS WILL IMPACT YOUR HOME

You will definitely want a space in your home for creating your gift baskets. You can work from a table that you erect and dismantle after each project, but the busier your business gets, the less you will want to do that. A clear dedicated workspace—where the family doesn't stack schoolbooks and magazines that you have to clean off each time you want to use it—will be a must. You'll also want it to be in a place where you can have shelves for commonly used supplies like twine, tape, and scissors. An unused room is the easiest, but it is also a great opportunity to clean up an area of the basement or a space in a large attic.

THINGS TO CONSIDER

You will need some sort of storage space to keep your supply of gift baskets and items to put in them. This is where it also pays not to go overboard in your purchasing—not only do you have to store all the stuff you purchase, but you will pay taxes on inventory that is hanging around. If you manufacture, produce, or sell goods to customers, inventory—a business asset—has tax implications. This can be complicated; be sure to have your tax accountant help you figure out logical levels of inventory and how to reduce and minimize any potential tax burdens.

You will need to get a good supply of baskets, but keep in mind that baskets can take up a lot of storage space.

If you choose to sell gift baskets to the general public, be prepared to be extremely busy around the major holidays—Thanksgiving, Christmas, Valentine's Day, and Mother's Day. Don't schedule large corporate orders around these key holidays or you will have more to do than you can handle. Also, stay away from perishable items in your baskets. You don't want items to go bad before you can use them.

HOW DO YOU WANT TO SPEND YOUR DAY?

The gift basket business offers a good variety of tasks to involve your day. Sometimes you will be completely absorbed in making baskets. Other times, you will be updating your website, generating invoices, or doing inventory updates.

But a lot of time you will be out shopping for items to put in your baskets. Or meeting with potential clients to show them what you can do. Or either delivering local baskets yourself or bringing packages to the post office or mailing center to ship out.

WHAT YOU WILL NEED

- **Marketing materials,** either brochures or websites or both.

- **Phone service.**

- **Computer system** (what you have already may be sufficient).

- **Inventory**: both of baskets and contents.

- **Supplies**: shred for the bottom of the baskets, gift tags, and cellophane to wrap them.

MARKETING ANGLE

The gift basket business can be marketed a number of ways. You can revolve your business around a specific market segment: women, children, men, parents, senior citizens, people with pets, NASCAR fans—the list is endless. Or you can focus on the holidays; several are prime gift-basket-giving occasions. Or you can target general markets, like corporations that might give gift baskets to clients, local and regional hospitals that would stock provide wellness and get-well gift baskets in their gift shops, or real estate agents that give gift baskets to new homeowners. You can also choose more than one of these markets, of course, but create marketing materials directed at each one individually. A brochure that contains information and basket selections directly toward the corporate world makes clients think that your business specializes in corporations.

NICE TOUCH

Perhaps you don't have a skill or product you make but someone you know does. You can purchase their soaps, baby bibs, crocheted mittens, or whatever and assemble a nice basket with a handmade flair.

EXPANSION POSSIBILITIES

If you want to remain a custom basket service, in order to expand you need to reach more and more clients for whom expense is no object. You can also combine a custom basket business with one that makes standard baskets—in the beginning, you will have time to make the baskets yourself that you sell at the hospital gift shop and the local pet shops. Once your higher-paying custom baskets really take off, you can hire someone to put together standard baskets according to your specifications.

WORDS TO KNOW

Anchoring: Securing items in a gift basket so they don't roll around.

FIFO: "First-in, first-out," an accounting system used to value inventory for tax purposes. Under FIFO, inventory is valued at its most recent cost.

Shred: The filler used to line the bottoms of baskets. Shred can be paper, tissue, cellophane, even wood shavings. Shred comes in many colors and textures.

RESOURCES

National Specialty Gift Association, nsgaonline.com

Gift Basket Review magazine, festivities-pub.com

Specialty Wraps, Etc. specialtywraps.com

3 CLEANING SERVICE

A cleaning service simply requires the desire and ability to get things sparkling clean! If you love keeping your own home and workspace spotless, you might be perfect for this business. There is no reason that a cleaning business can't be operated right from home.

Start by scouring all the books on cleaning tips you can find. Being armed with little tricks of the trade for cleaning a myriad of things is a great way to impress clients. Computer keyboards, wooden shutters, and other items with nooks and crannies and odd shapes are all things that most people avoid cleaning. Details like this can really make a difference in making a place appear clean and spotless.

There are many directions you can take this business. If you want to work during hours when no one else does, you can focus on office clients. The most effective way of doing that is to approach offices in office buildings where you can service many clients without traveling.

You can focus on retail businesses and keep your customers clumped into one or two blocks. Retail businesses may want to do their own daily vacuuming and trash removal, but you can offer a weekly service where you really scour the place.

Restaurants are in great need of daily thorough cleaning and can be a great source of steady clients. Restaurants that focus on breakfast and lunch can be cleaned in late afternoon and those that are dinner establishments can be cleaned in the morning or early afternoon before the restaurant opens its doors.

Perhaps you would be more interested in house cleaning. Many two-income families don't have the time for housecleaning and would love to come home to a tidy, clean, sweet-smelling home. Many times with cleaning services you don't have to spend lots of money on advertising or marketing because your customers will come by word of mouth. When Joan and Dave go to a party and exclaim to their friends how great it is to arrive home from a long day at work to a clean house, before you know it, those friends will be calling you to try out your cleaning service.

HOW THIS BUSINESS WILL IMPACT YOUR HOME

Since most of the work of a cleaning service is done on site, this business has little impact on your home. You will need a space for a computer workstation to keep track of your schedule, do your billing, and keep your financial records. You may want a space to store your equipment, unless you have a designated vehicle for the business in which the equipment can live. You probably want to have a storage space—just a rack of shelves will do it—to keep some supplies like paper towels and cleaning agents, since you will get a better price if you buy these things in bulk.

THINGS TO CONSIDER

If you go the corporate route, with the goal getting lots of customers in one building, you should plan on having to work evenings or very early mornings before office personnel arrive. This can be a great job for you if you have children and the other parent works a regular work day.

Cleaning products can be hard on the skin. Consider jumping on the "green" bandwagon and cleaning with environmentally friendly products. You will do your own health a favor and you can promote this as a marketing angle to potential clients.

HOW DO YOU WANT TO SPEND YOUR DAY?

If you don't get lots of clients in one concentrated area—like a multi-unit office building or block of retail stores or suburban housing complex— you will spend a good deal of time driving around from client to client.

WHAT YOU WILL NEED

- **Cleaning products.**

- **Cleaning tools:** Mops, dusting tools, and a vacuum cleaner (don't forget bags!) for those places that don't supply one.

- **Cleaning supplies:** Paper towels, cloth towels, chamois cloths, and rubber gloves to protect your hands.

- **Work Clothes:** A uniform or at least a nametag or embroidered shirt that identifies who you are.

- **Reference books:** Resources that will supply information on removing unusual stains or cleaning special surface materials.

- **A reliable vehicle:** Basic trasportation to get you to your clients. It can be your personal vehicle to start, but you'll need enough room to bring along a few long-handled cleaning tools. Get plastic handled tubs to store your different supplies so you can easily take them out of the vehicle when you need your vehicle for personal use.

MARKETING ANGLE

First, decide if you want to concentrate on a certain segment for your cleaning services. Office buildings? Restaurants? Homes? Then target your marketing materials to that group.

For office buildings, you will make money more efficiently if you target large buildings owned by one owner who leases out dozens of office spaces. Send or bring your marketing materials or presentation to the owners of those buildings.

Homeowners can be targeted in places where busy homeowners go, such as the bulletin board at the grocery store or favorite local restaurants.

Restaurants can be approached individually. Because of the differences in their schedules, you may be able to take on restaurants and/or offices, whose cleaning you will do either first thing in the morning or at night, along with a few homes to do during the day.

NICE TOUCH

Using environmentally friendly cleaning products can help you stand out from the crowd. It's good for the environment and healthier for you too!

For home cleaning services, find a florist with whom you can establish a relationship and get a good price on a small bouquet to leave on the kitchen counter with your bill. (Maybe you can trade a weekly cleaning service with them for a week's supply of cut flowers!) Pick up a supply of inexpensive glass vases at a dishware outlet store or dollar store; your customers will learn to leave the empty vase on the counter for your next visit! Just make sure to factor in these costs when figuring out your fees.

EXPANSION POSSIBILITIES

The best way to expand in this business is to subcontract to people to do some cleaning for you. You can become the marketer, scheduler, cost and quality controller, and perform other behind-the-scenes tasks, while others do most of the actual cleaning.

WORDS TO KNOW

Franchise: A "chain" of businesses where each member in the chain is independently owned and run but works within a standard set by the franchise. In exchange for some marketing and other types of backing, each member gives the franchise owner a percentage of revenue.

Organic stains: Stains caused by natural or nonchemical substances such as blood or grass, as opposed to chemicals such as oil or paint.

OSHA: The Occupational Safety and Health Administration; a federal agency that enforces health and safety laws particularly as they pertain to workplaces.

RESOURCES

GreenPeople (list of natural cleaners), greenpeople.org

Merry Maids, merrymaids.com, the ultimate in home cleaning franchises

Cleaningtips.com

CONSULTANT

4

To be a consultant, you need to have an expertise in something so you can market yourself as an advisor to others looking to work in that area. Typically, you will want to have hands-on experience in the field in which you are offering consulting services; that is why consulting is often a retirement business. Perhaps you managed several large warehouses in your career with a drugstore company, or you did all the marketing for many years for a large shoe manufacturer, or you set up a chain of beauty supply shops or take out restaurants. Maybe, over the years, your job as a travel agent gave you tremendous insight into the tourism industry. You can use this experience to help others do similar things without making the same mistakes that you made along the way.

A common consulting business is consulting about business itself! You can consult for potential startups, other homebased business wanna-be-owners, or for businesses who feel like their business has slowed down for no apparent reason.

You can be a career consultant and help people climb the ladder and establish a solid resume. If you have fashion experience, you can be a consultant to help someone learn how to dress for success. You can consult with people on how to launch their acting career, how to get patents on inventions—the list truly is endless.

Consulting is one of the most broad business ideas there is, but establishing yourself as a consultant is a slow process. It is difficult to start consulting while you are still working for a company since it would most likely be perceived as a conflict of interest and potentially a venue for giving away company secrets. But you can start putting out feelers while still employed.

Whatever consulting business you start, be prepared to be very up to date on your knowledge of the business. You will need to be aware of the business environment in general and the environment of the particular business in which you are consulting. Read all the financial newspapers regularly, subscribe online to financial blogs, put financial web sites in your favorites list and check in on them frequently. If you can't listen to the financial shows on NPR and other stations, subscribe to their podcasts and listen to them in your car as you drive to appointments or plug in and listen while you are working out. To consult in business, you have to saturate yourself with business news.

Then do all the same for the specific business you are in; subscribe to industry periodicals, blogs and podcasts, and bookmark appropriate websites. Plan to go to meetings, conferences, seminars, and trade shows—the places where you might find potential clients.

Starting a consulting business takes very little in terms of startup capital. You want to have a comfortable and well-equipped home office where you can do lots of research and phone conferencing. You can use your personal vehicle to get to clients; just be sure to keep a travel log.

HOW THIS BUSINESS WILL IMPACT YOUR HOME

You will most likely do face-to-face client work at your client's location, so you probably don't need to consider having clients come to your home. However, you will want a comfortable workstation since you will be doing a lot of work on the computer; from writing reports to research on the internet. Depending on your home life, this may mean a separate room for your work station, file cabinets, and to close the door on a ringing phone and fax machine during your off hours.

THINGS TO CONSIDER

A consulting business will only be successful if you have lots of experience and expertise in an area where other people have interest.

HOW DO YOU WANT TO SPEND YOUR DAY?

Consulting can be a great business for someone who likes being around people all the time but also enjoys some quiet time. You need to be out there meeting with clients and potential clients and often with their business associates and employees. But you also need to spend a good bit of time locked away in your office doing research and writing reports that will outline your recommendations. Consulting provides a nice balance of being on the go and being settled.

WHAT YOU WILL NEED

To have a successful consulting business, you need a long list of contacts to approach. They may not have anything to hire you for, but each contact knows dozens more contacts that are potential clients.

You will also need a good computer and a high speed internet connection. The internet is today's tool for keeping abreast of business news, trends, ideas, and fads. Set that computer up in a comfortable office with an ergonomic desk and desk chair, since you will be spending a lot of time there doing research.

MARKETING ANGLE

If you are an industry expert who retired after many years in the field in which you are consulting, flaunt it! Let everyone know you've been there, done that—and that your years of experience, successes as well as failures, can help them avoid the pitfalls and get to the successes easier and faster. Be sure all marketing materials you create, including your website, outline your experience. Emphasize that you have industry contacts. If you have been out of the field for a while, make sure you outline how you are keeping up with changes and current trends in your field of expertise.

NICE TOUCH

One consulting business idea is to pick up on the "green" trend. Helping businesses see where they could be more environmentally conscious— from recycling to using organically or locally grown materials—and then helping them to spread the word is a consulting possibility with lasting potential.

EXPANSION POSSIBILITIES

You could take on other consultants as subcontractors and expand your reach beyond your region or give them the local region if you like to travel. Another way to bring in more money with a consulting business is to add public speaking and seminars to your mix of services. In this way you can reach lots of people at once and potentially gain new consulting clients.

WORDS TO KNOW

Independent contractor: A person hired to do work for a company who is not employed by the company and does not fall under federal income withholding laws. Consultants are usually independent contractors.

Reclassification: The IRS can review an independent contractor or consultant's work and decide they are really W-2 employees. It is important to maintain independent status so that the employer only own the final results, not the method by or place in which the work is done.

RESOURCES

Consulting Magazine, consultingmagazine.com

Clarkston Consulting, clarkstonconsulting.com

The Consultant's Consultant, consultantsconsultant.com

5 EVENT PLANNING

Are you highly organized? Do you love to plan parties? Are you always the one to suggest that the family gathering take place at your home? Or the one to raise your hand to volunteer to coordinate the office holiday party? If so, an event-planning business might be perfect for you.

As with other businesses, you can focus on corporate clients; you'll be planning conferences, award ceremonies, and retirement events for businesses, and you'll probably get more money for your time. Or you can be an event planner for personal parties such as bar or bat mitzvahs, birthday celebrations, weddings and engagement parties, wedding showers, rehearsal dinners, etc.

One of the first things you need to do is visit every potential event location with whom you plan to work. Work with the marketing manager to tour each site and learn what is available at each location—does the venue offer meal service or do you need to use a caterer? What other services are available on site? What makes this place special?

Start a database that will allow you to sort venues by varying features—the number of people each site holds, if there is AV equipment is available on site, will you need to arrange for rental chairs, etc. Then when you are beginning to plan an event with a client, you can find out what the key parameters are for the event—300 people for a sit-down dinner—and easily pull up the three or four sites that meet the basic criteria.

It would be easy to focus just on wedding planning—enough so that it has its own entry later on. Wedding expenses are in the tens of thousands these days, so parents are often willing to pay someone like you to spend the time planning the details of the event while mom goes shopping with her daughter for a wedding dress. You may fully enjoy wedding planning and become an expert at it, or you may get bored planning the same kind of event all the time. This is where your own personality comes into play in choosing the types of events in which you might like to specialize.

HOW THIS BUSINESS IMPACTS YOUR HOME

Event planning is the kind of business where you may want to have a home office that is set up for clients to come visit. It's easier to have all your literature, product brochures, and portfolios of your events in one place than to have to carry all of that around to the client and risk forgetting an important book at home.

If you do have a home office for your event planning that clients will visit, be sure that:

- your home is in a pleasant location that clients will feel comfortable visiting

- your office reflects your high sense of style and gives the client the feeling that you will give the same kind of care to their event

- your neighborhood is zoned to permit this kind of homebased business

- your homeowner's insurance policy includes a business rider that covers client visits

- the entrance to your home office is welcoming, with landscaping, pathways, and lighting, and is preferably separate from the personal entrance to your home.

THINGS TO CONSIDER

You need to do a lot of running around to be an event planner. A small percentage of your time—maybe 25 percent—will be spent in your office. You will be visiting venues, checking up on the caterer, and you will probably need to be on site for the event itself, at least for the first half of it, to make sure everything is going as planned. You will need to be prepared to spend a lot of time talking with people, both in person and on the phone.

HOW DO YOU WANT TO SPEND YOUR DAY?

If you prefer to spend your day working alone and quietly doing research, this is probably not the homebased job for you.

WHAT YOU WILL NEED

As with most businesses these days, you will need a basic computer setup with printer, internet access, and a comfortable work station. You will need stylish and professional work clothes to wear to meet with clients— everything is about appearances in business. You will need a vehicle, which can certainly be your personal vehicle as long as it is appropriate.

MARKETING ANGLE

Like photography or consulting, the marketing of an event planning business is most successful when you focus on a particular market segment, like wedding, anniversary, or corporate product releases. If you plan to do any or all of these events, be sure to create different brochures for different market segments. You can then send out targeted brochures to potential clients outlining services specific to the services they will most likely need.

NICE TOUCH

In a business like event planning, word of mouth is key to getting more business. You want to leave your clients talking about what a great event it was—and thanks to you. Be sure to follow up with them with a letter saying that you hoped they enjoyed the event and that it was everything they wanted it to be—and if so, might they pass along these business cards you've enclosed to anyone they know who might need your services?

It's those little things that will have clients talking about how great it was to work with you. Little touches like unusual party favors for the wedding guests, or a gift basket sent to the mother of the bride two days before the wedding saying, "Hope you're holding up!" These thoughtful touches extend your reach beyond the event at hand.

EXPANSION POSSIBILITIES

You may decide to focus on one kind of event to start. Then, you can expand by branching out into other kinds of events that complement the type of event you have come to excel at.

WORDS TO KNOW

A/V Equipment: Any audio/visual equipment that may be needed for the event. Equipment may include microphones, a stereo system, a digital camcorder, or computer for PowerPoint presentations.

Master of Ceremonies: The MC plays host of the event. At a wedding reception, a DJ might serve as the MC, telling people when a toast is coming up or that the bride and groom will be having the dance floor to themselves for the first dance, etc.

Officiant: A priest, rabbi, judge, minister, or justice of the peace as well as other official figures who will "officiate" at an event, i.e., be the legal representative that performs a wedding service.

RESOURCES

EventRegister, thriva.com

Event planning tips, bonjourevents.com

Career info at dailyplan-it.net

HERBAL FARM STAND 6

Locally grown products are the wave of the future. People are looking for food that is grown closer to home, thus requiring less fuel for transport. Consumers want more information about how their food is grown and what kinds of chemical fertilizers and pesticides are used, and they also want to support the local economy.

Herbs are beautiful, useful, and easy to grow. They don't take up a lot of space and most can do well without a lot of fuss and attention. If you have a sizeable patch of land that is open to gardening, growing herbs can be approached in a few different ways. Your patch of land doesn't need to be enormous to grow herbs.

Of course, the more you can grow, the more you can sell, and the more money you can make. But a lot depends on what you do with the final product. You need to decide whether you will sell your herbs as live plants, picked or cut in bunches and packed, or dried. To sell live plants, it is best to plant them in the pots in which you will sell them, rather than putting them through the shock of transplantation twice—once from your garden to the pot and then from the pot to the purchaser's garden.

If you plan to market to cooks instead of gardeners, you will want to sell your herbs either fresh cut and packed in sealed bags, or dried and sold in baggies. You can also consider a "pick-your-own" arrangement, which is popular these days and saves you work; however, be aware that herbs are more delicate than most P.Y.O products. You may save your garden a lot of strife and your plants a lot of wear and tear if you do the picking.

Be sure to display your herbs for sale in an attractive stand or shed. Clean the dirt off the pots after you transplant the plants. Make sure to pull out weeds and straggling grass. Give your transplanted herbs a good watering. And create tags with transplanting and care instructions so that the herb's new owner can grow the herb successfully.

If you are selling dried or fresh cut herbs for culinary use, include some ideas for use or even recipes, in order to entice people to buy the herbs and be able to use them without having to do research themselves. This can add the impulse purchaser to the customers who come to your herb stand with a list of herbs for a particular recipe.

HOW THIS BUSINESS IMPACTS YOUR HOME

Depending on the size of your property, you may end up using substantial amount of space for your herb garden. As mentioned above, you can sell your herbs in a farm stand along the side of the road or you can sell them somewhere else like the nursery down the road or the farmer's market in the bank parking lot on Saturday morning—it's up to you (and your local zoning laws) whether you have customers coming to your home or not.

THINGS TO CONSIDER

For those in the northern parts of the country, this is going to be a seasonal endeavor. Even if you decide to grow your herbs in the summer and then spend the winter making dried arrangements, etc. you will still only be making money on your products during part of the year.

If you choose to sell to a greenhouse or nursery that will then in turn sell your herbs to their customers, you need to be prepared to take as much as half the price for them as you would if you sold them directly to the customer yourself. This works best if you have a large amount of herbs to sell.

HOW DO YOU WANT TO SPEND YOUR DAY?

To be a professional gardener you need to enjoy being outdoors and not mind getting your hands and clothes dirty—perhaps even swatting a few flies. You'll also need to enjoy the sales process; you will need to either deal with customers who are coming to your garden or booth at the farmer's market to purchase their plants, or with vendors where you sell your herbs.

WHAT YOU WILL NEED

You will need a patch of land that will hold the size of garden you want—or barring that, you can often rent a garden space in a community plot, although you may find you may soon outgrow that space.

If you are a good gardener but need to know more about specialty plants and how to grow them, consider taking a class or two to help you ensure your planting success.

You will need gardening tools. Do yourself a favor and get nice tools with ergonomic handles. If you love gardening, you already know the joy of working with the right high quality tools.

To prepare your garden, you may need to bring in loam and other amendments. Consider raised beds, which are neat looking and easier to manage. And you will need seeds of the various herbs you plan to grow.

Depending on the size of your business and whether you set up to sell from your home or take your herbs elsewhere, you may want a small pickup truck to transport your plants. If you choose to sell plants, you will need containers and also identification tags that provide plant care and transplanting instructions. If you decide to sell fresh clipped herbs, you will need a refrigerator, plastic bags, and adhesive labels that you can use with your computer to print out the name of the herb.

MARKETING ANGLE

Once you decide whether you are going to sell mostly fresh plants to gardeners or fresh picked and dried herbs to chefs, then you can create targeted marketing materials. If you are going for the gardener market, post notices for your herbs in places like restaurant bulletin boards or hardware stores. If you are going for the cooking market, investigate whether there is a cook's newsletter in the area or if someone gives cooking classes. You could also target your fresh-picked herbs to area high-quality restaurants who would love to promote that their meals are prepared with local fresh herbs.

NICE TOUCH

Any agricultural venture can enhance their image by going organic. Although it takes a long time and often a lot of expense to be certified organic, you can promote the fact that you use natural pest-deterring measures instead of pesticides, and only organic fertilizers to grow your herbs. This will matter a lot if you sell your herbs to people who plan to cook with them.

If you decide to sell clipped herbs specifically for cooking, consider adding a recipe or two to the package. Consider selling herbed vinegars and oils in addition to the fresh herbs themselves. Better yet, sell the herbs already in a container with instructions on how buyers can make their own herbed oils and vinegars.

EXPANSION POSSIBILITIES

You could start slowly with selling just herbs from a makeshift table with an honor box outside your home. From there, you could expand to selling to several farmers markets. You could then begin to market to restaurants and keep yourself busy most of the growing season supplying those two venues. If you have the space to grow enough herbs, you could expand your selling season by drying herbs in the fall and making herbal-flavored oils and vinegars to sell as gifts for the holidays. You could find a local retail outlet that might be willing to carry your products or perhaps a gift basket business that might be interested in designing a basket around your bottled herbal vinegars and oils. Because herbs have long been used for medicinal purposes and are often valued for healing properties, a specialty line of herbal remedies is a business direction to consider.

WORDS TO KNOW

Ag-Tourism: Short for "agricultural tourism," these are agricultural businesses that have created an agricultural destination point for tourists with things like hay rides, farm stands, maple syrup production, etc.

Culinary: Cooking related. Herbs used for flavoring food are referred to as "culinary usage."

PYO: "Pick your own." At a PYO farm, customers pick their own fruit or vegetables right out of the orchard or garden. Also known as "you pick" farms.

RESOURCES

GardenGuide.com offers information on growing herbs.

The North Carolina Extension Service has a great list of herbs with information on their space and light requirements, how to grow them, and what to use them for at ces.ncsu.edu/hort/hil/hil-8110.html.

Check your local Cooperative Extension for information on resources in your area. See www.csrees.usda.gov/Extension.

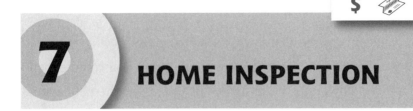

7 HOME INSPECTION

The home inspection business can take advantage of new home construction or a busy period of sales of existing homes where people are buying and selling homes at a rapid rate, all of which need inspecting in order for mortgages to be written.

You will generally work a regular work day in the home inspection field. During an especially up market you may find that day to be more like a 7am to 6pm work day, depending on daylight, with a few Saturdays thrown in there as well.

In order to be successful, you will want to establish contacts with real estate agents who can recommend your services to customers. The homebuyer retains your services and you provide them with a thorough and honest assessment of the home—from structural considerations like dry rot and poor construction to smaller details like whether the dishwasher is in good working condition.

Home inspection can be a very rewarding occupation. You are helping potential homeowners make a wise choice in selecting their new home. Or if you decide to go into commercial inspection, you can help people make wise investments.

The home inspection field is one where you will need to do constant updating of your education and knowledge. New products are constantly coming out on the market—if you only know about decks made of wood, you will not know how to inspect and assess the new materials on the market, such as composites that are made to look like real wood. Also keep apprised of all safety updates of materials and issues with things like off-gassing, carbon monoxide production, and other chemical precautions.

HOW THIS BUSINESS IMPACTS YOUR HOME

A good portion of home inspection work occurs away from your own home. One thing you will need is a safe space to store your vehicle, since it will have expensive tools and equipment in it that you won't want to take out at the end of the day and put back in before you take off in the morning. You will need a small office space for your computer and printer, but this can easily be a corner of the living room.

A cell phone with a good voice mail is essential since you will be on the road most of the time. Cell service can still be spotty in some areas, so voice mail can ensure that you don't miss a call from a potential client.

THINGS TO CONSIDER

You need to be in decent physical shape to be a home inspector. Inspecting a home can mean scrambling through small window-sized openings into crawl spaces that you can inspect only on your knees. You need to climb ladders, stairs, and into attics. If you have bad knees or a bad back, you probably won't want to be a home inspector.

Be sure to take into consideration the time you will need to spend on a computer creating the lengthy and detailed reports your customers expect.

HOW DO YOU WANT TO SPEND YOUR DAY?

If you are knowledgeable about home repair and don't mind working alone, home inspection may be the homebased business for you. You will need to spend quite a bit of time on a computer generating your inspection reports unless you hire someone to do that part of the work for you. However, you may find that the notes you take in the field are too cryptic to pass off to someone else to complete; this may be a task best done by you.

WHAT YOU WILL NEED

In order to inspect homes, you will need a vehicle that can accommodate a few tools, the most cumbersome of which will be a substantial ladder. You'll need either a truck or a van with a roof rack.

You also need to be bonded, a type of "trustworthy" insurance that insures to your client that you can be trusted to wander around a private home, many of which will still have occupants.

You definitely need a computer to create your reports. You can print out blank reports to carry with you and fill out by hand as you inspect the property, which you then either input into the computer yourself or hire someone to do that work for you. Or you can carry a laptop computer that allows you to do this on site.

Another expense will be for home inspection courses. You can attend initial multi-day training session that might run as much as $2,000. There are also home study courses, which may be sufficient particularly if you have background and experience in a related field. The American Society of Home Inspectors is the certifying organization for this field.

MARKETING ANGLE

The biggest marketing angle you can have with home inspection is to be absolutely thorough. Home buyers are handing out checks like candy during the home buying process, many times for things that they don't understand and that they think have no direct benefit to them (like points and title searches and mortgage insurance). When they hand you payment for your home inspection services, be sure they walk away feeling like they really got something for their money.

Also, always make it clear that you are offering your unbiased view of the condition of the home and all its systems—you have no conflict of interest with the bank, the real estate agent, the current owner, or the potential buyer. In the end, no one is going to make out if you lean your inspection to favor one party or another—the current owner may be happy to have made the sale without a glitch but if a problem arises, you and they could be facing a lawsuit. The lender is not going to be happy if the new buyer can't afford to fix something significant and walks away from the property. And the new buyer won't be recommending your services to anyone else if you didn't point out a major consideration in the home.

NICE TOUCH

Find reliable sources of information and include copies of these findings (with permission from the copyright holder) with your reports regarding things that came up during your inspection. Perhaps your inspection revealed that the furnace is about ready to head to the scrap yard—an article or two comparing different furnace types is well appreciated by customers.

Another thing you might do is offer one or two follow-up phone calls to help them with any questions they have as they address the problems that you may have uncovered.

EXPANSION POSSIBILITIES

The most common expansion of home inspection services is to branch out from home inspection to commercial and industrial real estate properties.

WORDS TO KNOW

GFCI: A "ground fault circuit interrupter" is an electrical safety outlet that has a built-in breaker that shuts the electricity to the outlet if it senses an electric problem. They are often required by code to be installed near any sink or other water source.

Narrative report: A lengthy and detailed report done by the home inspector and give to the homeowner or whomever contracted the inspection.

Radon: A naturally occurring radioactive gas that can leak into a home from the ground. Radon has been suspected to be cancer causing, and many home inspections include installation of a radon detection kit that shows the radon level in the home and indicates whether radon-blocking installations should be recommended.

RESOURCES

American Society of Home Inspectors, ashi.com

National Association of Home Inspectors, nahi.org

HOME ENERGY AUDITOR 8

A ll homeowners are always on the lookout for ways to save on their utility bills. You can come to their aid by providing them with an audit of their house and giving them a breakdown of how they could accomplish real savings in heating, cooling, and electrical use. You can go one step further and do the implementation and installation of some of your suggestions in their home yourself.

A huge part of your audit will be on the actual heating and cooling systems. Determine how efficient the client's current system is and give them information on how they can either make it more efficient, or what would be a good replacement system. There are lots of areas where you can be helpful, from ductwork maintenance and reconfiguration, to changing the electrical heating zones or how the homeowners use certain rooms. For instance, if a homeowner is going to back up their oil-fired furnace with a woodstove, if they install the woodstove in the room where the furnace thermostat is, the rest of the house will be undesirably cold since the woodstove heat is telling the thermostat that the house is warm enough even though it may be only that room. Homeowners can benefit from your unique perspective.

Once they have an efficient heating and cooling system in place, you'll want to make sure the warm and cool air aren't leaking out of the house. Go through the entire house and conduct something similar to a home inspection. Figure out how well insulated the house is and whether there is warm air escaping through window frames, doorsills, and outside wall electrical outlets. Check the efficiency of the windows themselves. Check the attic—if there is no whole house fan, recommend one for keeping the house cooler in summer.

You will want to inspect all caulking and insulation to make sure that the house is being well protected, and that insulation that your customer thought was taking care of things isn't either settled (in the case of the once-popular blow-in insulation) or being used primarily for rodent nesting.

Another huge area of home energy use is appliances. Do a complete appliance audit, with efficiency ratings and calculations based on the age of the appliance. And don't forget the water heater!

HOW THIS BUSINESS IMPACTS YOUR HOME

You should not need to keep much in the way of supplies at your home nor will you need to have customers come to your home for any reason. The biggest impact this business will have on your home is the usual need for a modest office with a computer work station—and even in that case, you probably want a laptop computer so you can take it along with you to take notes and create a report for the homeowner as you go.

THINGS TO CONSIDER

Create a form that consists mostly of a checklist of everything you want to inspect while you are at the home. If you bring your laptop along, fill in this form as you do the inspection.

HOW DO YOU WANT TO SPEND YOUR DAY?

You will definitely be getting dirty, crawling around in basements and crawl spaces, maybe even up in attics and on roofs. You will need to climb a ladder with almost every job you take on. Be sure you are in the physical condition to do this.

WHAT YOU WILL NEED

You will need a solid understanding of home energy use and building construction. Also learn the energy star rating system for appliances and what that means. You'll need some basic tools; don't forget a good flashlight and a tape measure. If you recommend that the homeowner replace a 20-year-old refrigerator to save on their electric bill, you should to give them the measurements they need to go to the appliance store and pick out what they want.

MARKETING ANGLE

The main marketing angle you need to take with this business is that the savings realized by reducing their heating, cooling, and electrical bills will more than make up the cost of hiring you and carrying out your recommendations. Secondarily, they will be helping the planet by lessening the amount of nonrenewable energy they use. They can reduce their carbon footprint—and save money too.

NICE TOUCH

When you are a consultant who sells or installs products, there is a chance of appearing to have a conflict of interest—you appear to recommend the only products you have for sale. Be honest and get a reputation for being fair-minded. Only recommend installation of products that will truly save the customer money; don't recommend them just because you sell them. And when you do think they should install something you sell, be sure to emphasize that the decision is theirs and theirs alone. You can also help alleviate their concerns by giving them literature or website information on other manufacturers of these products so they can do their own consumer research and decide which product they want to go with—

yours or someone else's. If they choose a product you don't sell, have a ready list of installers or numbers for them to easily arrange purchase and installation.

EXPANSION POSSIBILITIES

If you decide to sell products, you can definitely see some savings with product sales and installation. Also, to expand in this business, you can market your services to businesses. Businesses like to see energy savings as much as homeowners, if not more so. And they are often able to be charged more than homeowners.

WORDS TO KNOW

Energy Star: A national program from the U.S. Environmental Protection Agency and Department of Energy that rates an appliance's energy usage and helps homeowners improve energy efficiency.

Insulation: Insulation is used in many places in the home to block air flow and prevent warmed air from leaking outside during winter and cooled air from leaking out of the home during summer. Insulation comes with an R-factor, which tells how insulative the particular type of insulation is.

Nonrenewable energy: Refers to fossil fuels like oil, gas, and coal, of which there is a finite amount stored in the earth.

RESOURCES

hes.lbl.gov, a do-it-yourself home energy audit

energysavers.gov

PERSONAL CONCIERGE 9

The concierge at a hotel can be an incredibly useful person. They know things that can help make your trip much more comfortable, efficient, or effective. This is also true of the personal concierge. Your job will be to make your client's life more efficient and help them be more effective.

Being the go-to person for someone who is busy makes you a very busy person yourself! If you can stand the time pressures that are often part of a personal concierge's life, this may be the perfect homebased business for you.

This business is for someone who is supremely efficient and has the ability to make things happen. People who hire you will expect things when they want them and you need to be able to come through with not only what they want, but with a personal touch and a smile on your face.

The most likely clients for a personal concierge service are top executives who find themselves at the office by 7 am and are there most nights until 9 pm, leaving them very little time to do all those things that often need to be done during those very hours.

The tasks you could be asked to do include purchasing personal gifts for your client's family, friends, or business associates; making lunch, dinner, or ski trip reservations; going grocery shopping; bringing the dog to the groomer; bringing the car through the car wash; booking the clown and ponies for a child's birthday party; or lining up a housecleaning service to get the client's home ready for an important dinner party. You could also find yourself doing things like racing to the airport to deliver something your client forgot, or searching for that specific gift just two hours before your client is scheduled to have an anniversary dinner.

You should plan to charge a base rate so that you have a monthly income you can count on. That rate can include certain common services, a list that should be tailored to meet that particular client's needs. Then add on fees for other kinds of work on top of your monthly base rate.

HOW THIS BUSINESS IMPACTS YOUR HOME

Although it isn't necessary, an efficient home office is very helpful in conducting your business as a personal concierge.

THINGS TO CONSIDER

As a personal concierge, you put yourself at the beck and call of your clients. You need to set the parameters of when you are available if you want to have any time of your own. And you need to have the right connections to get wealthy clients who can pay you enough for this service in order to keep the number of clients you have at a manageable level.

HOW DO YOU WANT TO SPEND YOUR DAY?

It is possible to be contacted any time by a client, so you never know what your day is going to look like. That can be great for some, disconcerting for others. Even though you may be very organized and like the idea of helping someone else be more efficient, think carefully about not being able to control this aspect of your day.

WHAT YOU WILL NEED

A home office would be nice, but the most important thing you need is a cellular phone. If your business line is a cell phone, be sure to have a hands-free earpiece in order to be able to search online as you are speaking to a client. And be sure your cell phone is loaded with a good list of contacts that you can call at a moment's notice for common things like flowers or numbers to your clients' favorite restaurants for last-minute dinner reservations. You will want high-speed internet access and at least a laptop computer.

MARKETING ANGLE

To find clients, you will need to go where the busy people are. Busy people who have the money for a personal concierge probably eat at expensive restaurants—i.e., the kind that don't have a cluttered bulletin board in the waiting area or use menus with business ads printed on them. Find out if local corporations might let you put a note in their newsletter. Perhaps a blog or column in a local newspaper that offers tips to busy people could trigger some business.

This service thrives on word of mouth, and once you have a client or two whose lives you transform and they extol your virtues at their workplace or to their friends and family, you will begin to see the customers roll in.

NICE TOUCH

The nicest touch a concierge can offer is follow up. Always make sure that what you thought you had arranged actually takes place. And be sure to check with your client that everything was satisfactory. In addition, it's important to be prepared. Create a database for each client with important dates, such as birthdays and anniversaries; preferences, such as favorite restaurants and destinations; and overall do's and don'ts.

EXPANSION POSSIBILITIES

You will only be able to take on so many clients before you need a personal concierge for yourself—which is just what you might consider. Once you are established, hire someone who can take some of the mundane tasks off your hands while you spend your time doing the things that you do best.

WORDS TO KNOW

Concierge: The term "concierge" is derived from the French phrase *comte des cierges,* which literally means "the keeper of candles." The person with this title attended to the whims of visiting noblemen at medieval castles. Concierges today fill the requests of clients or hotel guests.

Membership fees: Some concierges collect membership fees, which allow clients a certain number of requests monthly.

Referral fees: Payments given by businesses to concierges for sending business to them.

RESOURCES

American Errand Runners Organization, errandinfo.com

National Concierge Association, conciergeassoc.org

PET SITTING

10

The American Pet Products Manufacturers Association 2005-2006 survey revealed that there are over 164 million cats and dogs kept as pets in the United States. Numbers rose significantly from the 2003-2004 survey and there is no indication that pet ownership will be slowing down. And this number doesn't include millions and millions of other small animals kept as pets such as hamsters, ferrets, birds, reptiles, and fish in fish tanks.

All of these animals will need care when their owners are away on vacations, business trips, and holiday travel. That's where you come in.

Starting a pet sitting service requires almost nothing in start-up costs. All you need is yourself. You do need some general credentials that will cost little or nothing to acquire.

A population that spends billions of dollars each year on pet-related products is also going to be very particular about whom they choose to take care of their precious pets. Your list of credentials should probably include personal pet ownership—if not currently, at least in the past—as well as other pet-related experience including working at a pet food store, an animal hospital, or other animal-related business.

You will also want to know a bit about animal medical care, especially emergencies. The Red Cross offers a pet first aid class that is very worthwhile for pet sitters to take. Check your local veterinarians or Red Cross chapter to see if a first aid class is offered in your area. You will end up with a certificate of completion that you can include in your portfolio to prove you took the class, and you can add that credential to your pet-friendly resume. In addition, you'll need to know how to find pet care in case of emergency; many communities have an emergency medical clinic that is available when vets are closed for the day.

You will need to spend a little to become "bonded." This is known as "honesty insurance," and ensures your clients that you won't get their house keys and make off with their valuables (or that they'll get their money back if you do).

Because of the number of clients you need to take on to make a decent living with petsitting, you need to be extremely organized. You can't forget even one appointment, because there is nothing that will end your petsitting business faster than word spreading that you neglected Fluffy or Bowser.

HOW THIS BUSINESS IMPACTS YOUR HOME

This low-key homebased business should have very little impact on your home. Unless you decide to take in animals for care in your own home—in which case you may run into some zoning problems or issues with your otherwise enthusiastic family members—the most you may need is space in your house to set up a computer and do the bookkeeping for your business, and a separate phone line with voice mail to make sure you catch incoming calls from potential customers.

THINGS TO CONSIDER

Pet care can be physically demanding. This is especially true if you decide to take on barn animals; cleaning stalls, moving hay, and toting wheelbarrows to the manure pile requires physical strength and stamina.

Even if you are just walking the family dog, many dogs are not obedience trained and don't walk on a leash very well. Even a 20-pound pooch can get tiring when they are dragging you down the sidewalk two or three times every day.

Be sure to be clear about what you require of the animals in your care. If you have some dog training experience, you don't need to give it away for free. Ask the owner if they would like you to work with their dog to teach it how to walk on a leash or be an all-round "canine good citizen." If they are hiring you for petsitting—especially if it is an ongoing job midday while they are at work—chances are they don't have the time to do this training themselves and would be happy to pay you to help them. But don't give it away for free! Be sure to charge for your time and training—and be prepared to prove that you have have the experience and credentials to train their dog.

Also, because none of us ever knows when an emergency may strike, it is important to have a backup person you can count on to help you out in a crisis. Perhaps you are stuck with a broken-down car or have a family emergency. People will be sympathetic, but they still want their pet to be cared for. Sending a backup will show that you are a responsible care giver.

HOW DO YOU WANT TO SPEND YOUR DAY?

Pet sitting can be a very time-intensive business. To get to any significant income levels, you need to take on several clients. This can chop your day up into pretty small pieces. If that isn't appealing to you, you can be more choosy about the jobs you take on—perhaps you only do weeklong vacation care, etc.—but petsitters will tell you that the midday dog walks are a big part of their income.

WHAT YOU WILL NEED

First, you need to love animals and have the patience and understanding to spend a lot of time with them!

Next, you'll need transportation. Although you won't need to run out and buy a new vehicle, the one you have must be reliable, and you should be able to transport pets in it, since some of your petsitting jobs may require that you take Rover to the park for a daily romp—rain or shine.

You will need a computer and printer to keep track of jobs, print out invoices, and go online for research. Set up a separate phone line or get a phone that will allow you to have a dedicated business line. And print business cards to distribute to your clients and post around town.

MARKETING ANGLE

You must be interested in pet sitting for a reason—you have had pets all your life, you are a licensed veterinary technician, or you can't have pets at the moment so you are doing this to enjoy others' pets. Get this across in all your marketing info. Be sure your marketing literature shows animals—people with pets love animals!

NICE TOUCH

Purchase an inexpensive digital camera and take photos of the pets under your care, showing them relaxing at home while their owners are away. Leave one or two prints with a note about how things went while they were gone along with your bill at the end of the job. Or if you have a regular job taking care of someone's pets midday, leave pictures once a week with your bill, showing the family dog having fun in the park or playing catch in the backyard. Pet owners hate leaving their pets and knowing that they are comfortable while their humans are away will endear you to them and give you work for a long time to come. And it will provide that best form of advertising—word of mouth—when they tell all their friends how great you are.

EXPANSION POSSIBILITIES

You could expand into many avenues related to pets; you could sell some pet products such as a line of food or pet accessories (toys, beds, collars, etc.), expand into general housesitting including pets rather than just pet sitting, open a boarding kennel, create a space in your home to do dog grooming—the possibilities are endless. If you aren't already licensed as a veterinary technician, consider going to school part time and getting your license or certification while you get your business up and running. This will allow you to take on more complicated pet sitting jobs, such as caring for a pet recovering from surgery while the owner is at work or pet sitting for a diabetic cat while the owner is on vacation. Be sure to charge more for your licensed credentials! Get endorsements from veterinarians that you work with and point out in your marketing literature exactly why it is worth paying more for your pet sitting services.

WORDS TO KNOW

Animal husbandry: The caretaking of animals.

First aid: The immediate critical care given to a wounded or injured animal or person.

Vital signs: Main signs of life, such as temperature, pulse, and respiration. All pet sitters should know the standard vital signs for all the types of animals in their care, and know how to check them.

RESOURCES

Pat Moran's Professional Pet Sitting Products, patmoran.com

Pet Sitter's International, petsit.com

11 EDITORIAL SERVICES

Do you have an English degree lurking in your background or do you simply have a way with words? There are many different types of editorial services that you can offer the world.

Depending on what you would like to do, you will want to consider taking some classes. This will give you the resume that clients will expect to see. Start small and build your clientele one job at a time until you have some experience to list along with your education.

Here are some of the editorial services you can provide from the quiet of your own home:

- **Copyediting.** Before a written piece is designed, it goes through a copyediting process. This is where fact checking takes place, and where grammatical, stylistic, and typographical errors are caught.

- **Proofreading.** This is the last stop for a "finished" piece, and where it is checked for any remaining spelling and grammatical errors before it goes to the printer or goes live on the web. This is also the stage where the piece is first presented in its final design, so it is checked for proper use of type styles, layout, spacing, etc. The proofreader makes sure the copyediting changes have been properly made and no new errors are created in the process. You need a keen eye for detail to be a proofreader.

- **Indexing.** Creating an index is a very specific and valuable skill. There are indexing courses available and you can get indexing software.

- **Developmental Editing.** This level of editorial work requires some experience in publication work. A developmental editor works with a manuscript on big-picture things like organization and content issues.

- **Book Doctoring.** This is an editorial service provided for manuscripts written by experts who know their field but don't necessarily know how to put a book together. They create a manuscript as best they can and then a book doctor puts it into publishable shape.

- **Ghost Writing.** Often a service provided to non-writing experts, ghost writing starts a level back from book doctoring. As a ghost writer, you actually do the research and write the book and someone else's name is attached as the author.

- **Copywriting.** Also known as business writing, this is writing that promotes a product or a service; it is provided to advertising agencies, public relations firms, and PR departments of large companies.

- **Book writing.** Writing books can be a reasonable way to make a living from your home. Do you have an expertise in something professional, such as accounting or interior decorating? Or personally, like knitting or do-it-yourself home improvement? Why not write a book about it?

- **Magazine article writing.** Magazines and newspapers are a great way to get your writing published before tackling the daunting task of writing a whole book. Again, you can write about professional or personal areas of expertise.

- **Web page content provider.** Providing content for a web site is a good way to make some money writing. Surf the web and find some web sites that you can approach with your expertise.

HOW THIS BUSINESS IMPACTS YOUR HOME

You will need a definitive office space to set up your work station. Depending on how you like to work and what your home environment is like, it can be important that you have a space that can be blocked off from the noise of the rest of the house.

Once you get this business up and running, you will probably be receiving deliveries several times per week from the couriers like FedEx, UPS, and DHL. Otherwise, you shouldn't have to consider having much in the way of business traffic to your home.

THINGS TO CONSIDER

Your computer will become your best friend. Be sure to create a comfortable, safe, and ergonomic space in which to work.

It will take a little while for you to establish yourself in this business so you need to be prepared to start off slowly. Have savings set aside to carry you until you are well established or start while you are still fully employed and do your editorial business on the side.

HOW DO YOU WANT TO SPEND YOUR DAY?

You will be spending a lot of time sitting in front of a computer. However, if you are working from home, there is no reason you can't get up every couple hours and go work in the garden or take a quick walk.

WHAT YOU WILL NEED

Your editorial services business will need a basic computer with a printer, and maybe a fax machine. Be sure to buy an ergonomic desk chair. Find some sources online to tell you how to set your office up ergonomically to avoid things like carpal tunnel syndrome or back problems.

MARKETING ANGLE

You can go in dozens of different directions when it comes to marketing an editorial services business. If you choose to focus on writing, you can direct your efforts toward book, magazine, or newspaper writing, providing web content, or writing marketing material—both web-based and print—for companies. Whatever angle you take, you will need to get some published work to promote yourself. So unless you start this business with a significant wealth of writing clips under your belt, you may need to do some work for free or at low rates to start.

If you choose to concentrate on the other kinds of editorial services, like proofreading, copyediting, or indexing, it will pay to take some courses, either online or at a college or other editorial-related school. You can approach the same types of places as for writing work—newspapers, magazines, books, online content providers or sites. Be absolutely sure that when you send out marketing materials, there isn't a single mistake in them!

NICE TOUCH

Research appropriate contests and submit your finished projects to them. Winning contests can add pizzazz to your resume, gives you a reason to send out a press release about your work, and gives a nice opportunity to get your client's name in the news as well.

EXPANSION POSSIBILITIES

This is a business where you can really start small with very little cash outlay except an upgraded computer system and the latest editions of the popular reference books (*The Chicago Manual of Style* and *Webster's Collegiate Dictionary*, for example). Anything you do from there is an expansion. This is also a case where there is only so much one person can do; if you get to the point where you are taking on significant amounts of work, more than you have time for, consider hiring someone a few hours a week to do some of the tasks that don't involve your key strength. Perhaps someone could do some of the research for a book or type out your field notes for articles, etc.

WORDS TO KNOW

Font: Traditionally defined as a complete character set of a single size of a particular typeface.

Typeface: A set of characters that includes uppercase and lowercase alphabetical characters, numbers, punctuation, and special characters.

Copyright: The legal right to reproduce, publish, and sell an artistic work. Be sure you hold copyright to everything you use in your printed materials (which is automatically yours upon creation) or that you get written permission to use it from the copyright holder.

Printing: The process of manufacturing a piece into a final form to be distributed. Publishers and printers are often thought of as one and the same, but typically the *publisher* finds the author, edits the manuscript, has the book layout designed and produced, and sends a digital file to a *printer*, who produces the book by printing it to paper and binding it into a cover.

RESOURCES

AP Style Guide, Associated Press

Chicago Manual of Style, chicagomanualofstyle.org

Copyediting certificate program, Emerson College, emerson.edu/ce/programs/certificate/Copyediting-Certificate.cfm

WEDDING PLANNER 12

Thinking up new ideas for weddings can be the most challenging and most fun part of being a wedding consultant. You will need to be up to date on wedding trends and fads, dress styles, color trends—almost everything under the sun! It can be a lot to keep up with but it can be exciting and fun, too!

Word of mouth is definitely important in this business. The happy bride will tell all of her friends about how great you were and how they have to use your services for their own weddings.

You can design your wedding consulting services however you want. Offer your customers an ala carte menu of services, from helping pick flowers, the wedding gown, and bridesmaid dresses, to picking the venue and hiring the caterer. If you do offer a selection of services, you will want to group them so that you are doing all the same type of service—for example, you don't want to be the one helping with the bridesmaid dresses while someone else is doing the tuxedos or the flowers. The quality of your service is reflected in all of these things.

The wedding business is clearly booming—according to the National Association of Wedding Ministers, an average of 2.4 million weddings are performed in the United States every year at an average cost of $22,000 each. Weddings are more spread out over the year than ever, with June and August still the most popular months.

You do not have to be married yourself to be a successful wedding planner. However, you do need to subscribe to every general wedding magazine on the planet and get to know the wedding business inside and out. Before you open your business, shop at all the wedding shops, and even pretend you are a bride-to-be to see what kinds of services the wedding gown shop provides and how they treat potential customers. Taste wedding cakes until you don't care if you have another piece of cake in your life! You need to know every detail of the business to give the accurate impression that you are the go-to person for anyone planning a wedding.

HOW THIS BUSINESS IMPACTS YOUR HOME

You can consult with your clients mostly at their own homes or at the wedding gown shop, caterer, or wherever the next item on your planning list takes you. So you don't necessarily need a home office. However, if your home lends itself to having an office where clients can come, that is a helpful thing. You can have all of your design books and samples right at your fingertips without having to tote everything around.

You do need to consider zoning and insurance when having clients come to your home. Also, because you are offering a service that is all about elegance and design, it is important that your home be a showcase for your own tastes. Clients need to walk to your door exclaiming how beautiful your home and landscaping is or they certainly aren't going to trust you to make their wedding the most beautiful one ever.

If you don't have clients coming to your home, you need just the usual home office space. You may need little extra storage space for all your sample dishware, menus, etc., unless you have a vehicle where you can store these all the time.

THINGS TO CONSIDER

You will be saturated in the wedding business as a wedding consultant. Flower bouquets and white dresses and catering will be on your mind all the time. If this sounds like heaven to you, you are definitely a candidate for this business!

HOW DO YOU WANT TO SPEND YOUR DAY?

Being a wedding consultant will mean doing a lot of running around. It will also mean being extremely busy during the classic May, June, and September wedding crunch times, and not as busy the rest of the year. Be sure you can handle that inconsistency in your workload.

WHAT YOU WILL NEED

While you will definitely need a computer work station and office, your biggest need will be to develop contacts in the area that your consulting business will cover. You need everyone in the most remote part of the wedding business to know you do wedding planning so they can recommend you to their clients.

MARKETING ANGLE

Being a wedding planner comes with its own built-in marketing angle. However, you can tailor your marketing from there as well. Perhaps you want to be wedding planner to the wealthy, helping affluent people choose custom wedding dresses and ceremony venues in posh places. Or maybe you would like to become known for planning innovative and creative weddings. Whatever you decide, make sure all your marketing materials reflects that angle. And place your materials in the right places— if you want to be the wedding planner to the stars, you won't find your clients by posting a sign at the grocery store.

NICE TOUCH

This seems obvious, but always be sure to send a wedding gift to the happy couple whose wedding you planned.

EXPANSION POSSIBILITIES

If you've ever watched the movie The Wedding Planner (and you should have if you are really serious about being a wedding planner!), you know that you can expand your empire into a law-firm like partnering scenario, bringing on other wedding planners who take on the markets you are not interested in. You can also expand by adding on to the menu of services you provide. Perhaps you start out by planning post-ceremony receptions. Then you add rehearsal dinners. By the time you have some experience in these areas, you can add choosing the color scheme, and picking out the wedding gown, the mother-of-the-bride gown, etc.

WORDS TO KNOW

Bomboniere: The Italian term for the favors that are given to wedding guests.

Ganache: An icing that is made from chocolate and heavy cream.

Nosegay: A small bouquet of flowers or herbs, carried by flower girls or bridesmaids.

RESOURCES

Professional Bridal Consultant course, Penn Foster Career School, pennfoster.edu

Wedding Planner course, uscareerinstitute.info

ACCOUNTANT

13

Many people dislike the numbers side of business. If you are one of those who finds numbers fascinating, you can have people ringing your phone off the hook for your services.

There are many facets to the accounting business that you can focus on. People who hire you will want to know that you have expertise or experience or somehow have gained knowledge about their area of business. It may be the specific industry they are in, the aspect of industry their business does (manufacturing, retail, service industry, for example), or even just small business vs. large corporation. Book authors, film actors, and others need to know that you understand the royalty income. Only you can decide which aspects interest you and which you may already have a leg up on.

Small business owners want to see that you either have run your own small business and understand their concerns from that perspective. Or that you have several other small business clients and have the same issues come up with these other of your clients—things like inventory concerns and how to finance growth.

Another aspect of small business that can become a niche for you is to specialize in financial reports for business plans. Start-up businesses create business and marketing plans to outline their business, prove to a bank they are worthy of financing, and to have an organized framework in which to run their business and measure their success against.

If you are already versed in the accounting field and are thinking about starting a homebased accounting business but are still employed outside the home, you might consider taking on a couple clients on the side (unless this is a conflict of interest with your current employment situation). This will help you start to build a clientele list to put on your resume.

Create a flier outlining your services. Before you do that, you need to know what those services will be. Do you want to simply do bookkeeping for a small business? That would involve balancing the business checkbook each month, keeping income and expense records, helping with travel logs including mileage and entertainment expenses—that kind of day-to-day thing.

A more involved level of accounting would be do actually work up balance sheets, income statements, and other financial reports on a monthly, quarterly, and/or annual basis, depending on the needs of the business.

Other specializations can include tax accounting, a huge area of potential work. Many business owners don't mind keeping their own day-to-day bookkeeping records but would rather get professional help with their taxes.

HOW THIS BUSINESS IMPACTS YOUR HOME

Doing accounting work is perfect business for the small home office, and the impact on the home can be minor. You won't need customers coming to you; in fact, it is better if you make a visit to their offices when you need to pick up paperwork or gather information. That way you get to know their business a little more each time and you can be sure they don't forget something you need. If they have to, there is always the mail or courier service to send something along.

You will, however, need some sort of office space exclusive to your business, preferably with a door you can shut. Accounting work should be done in peace—you don't want to try to work with a company's numbers in the corner of the living room while your kids are playing around.

THINGS TO CONSIDER

You really need to love working with numbers and financial statements of all kinds to do this work. If you do not have enough current experience or education to start a business but believe this is something you would like to consider, take a couple classes and find out if this work is for you. It won't be wasted—if you decide you love it, you'll be on your way to gaining educational credentials with a couple classes already under your belt. If you decide you can't imagine spending all your time crunching numbers, think of the years of misery or the expense of an aborted business that you will save yourself just for the cost of a couple classes.

HOW DO YOU WANT TO SPEND YOUR DAY?

These days, being an accountant means spending your time at a computer. Oh, there could be a few moments of the day spent jotting numbers on a pad of paper, but for the most part your fingers will be dancing across the number pad of the computer keyboard and the calculator keys.

You will have those times when you are meeting with clients to go over the financials or gathering information to create them. But this amounts to less time than you will spend sitting at your desk. Don't forget that the beauty of homebased businesses is that you can get up out of your chair and take a walk around the block, a run through the park, or plant a few fall bulbs any time you want!

WHAT YOU WILL NEED

As mentioned earlier, if you don't have work history that gives you financial expertise—and sometimes even if you do—you will definitely want to take a few classes and even consider getting a two-year degree. You will need a basic computer system, a comfortable workstation with excellent lighting, and desk space to spread out paperwork.

MARKETING ANGLE

Even accounting can have a marketing angle! You can choose to do accounting work for individuals, for small business, or for larger businesses. What you decide will have an impact on where you advertise for clients. Individuals and small businesses may be targeted by placing an ad on a local restaurant menu. Small and larger business clients can be marketed to by networking at events put on by the local chamber of commerce and other business resource groups. You need to go where the clients are that you would like to conduct business with.

NICE TOUCH

A nice touch, and one that will gain you business when your current clients tell all their friends, is to go the extra mile to learn about your existing or prospective client's area of business. If warehousing inventory is part of a client's business, ask to get a tour of the warehouse. Learn the reality of how they do things; it shows you are interested in their business and helps you to offer useful ideas for curbing costs in the future.

EXPANSION POSSIBILITIES

If you start out doing simple accounting and bookkeeping, you can expand your business by adding services. Services such as tax accounting can be more highly skilled and therefore you can charge more for these services. If you just add on services to what you already offer and you already have your maximum number of clients, you will need to consider having an employee who can help you with simple bookkeeping while you concentrate on the higher-paying accounting. Or you can take on someone who already knows the higher-skilled accounting and expand by taking a share of the work that he or she does. And doing this doesn't mean you have to give up the homebased aspect of your business—perhaps this employee, partner, or subcontractor wants to work at home as well, and you meet once/week to discuss common clients or other business concerns.

WORDS TO KNOW

Gross Margin: The ratio of gross profit to sales revenue. For a retailer, it is the markup of the retail over the wholesale price.

Near-cash assets: Assets that can be converted to cash in a short period of time.

Unresolved equity: A term that refers to the difference between total assets and total liabilities on the balance sheet. The balance sheet should show total assets is equal to total liability plus equity.

RESOURCES

Villanova University, Tulane University, and Florida Tech are just one of many schools that offer online accounting services associate's level degrees. Check schools.online-education.net for a full list.

14 TAX PREPARER

As previously mentioned, you can start a homebased financial business in tax preparation. You will need not only an accounting-related degree and experience, but you will also need to get tax-specific training.

Check the IRS for what they offer. Also, working for tax preparation companies like H&R Block can give you the experience and work history you need to start your own tax preparation business. Most tax preparation franchises offer courses, seminars, and training to get you ready to work for them. You will learn a lot about tax preparation while working for them before going out on your own. Lots of people take part-time jobs working for tax preparers during the busy tax season between the first of the year and the infamous April 15th.

Like accounting, you should plan to specialize either in personal tax work, tax prep for small businesses, or tax preparation for large corporation (the latter often have their own tax and accounting experts). Whatever field you choose to specialize in, you need a great under-standing of all tax implications for that particular group.

Specializing in small business allows you to become proficient at helping small businesses utilize legitimate deductions. You will be called on to help in the growth of the company, pointing out the tax implications of certain expansions, such as tax on inventory or real estate.

You will also want to become very familiar with state tax laws in your own as well as neighboring states.

Tax preparation can be interesting and lucrative work. There is a lot of educational support out there to learn tax preparation and all its complexities. And there are lots of individuals and businesses willing to spend a few hundred dollars a year to have someone else prepare their taxes and keep watch for tax breaks or tax burdens on their behalf.

HOW THIS BUSINESS IMPACTS YOUR HOME

Like with an accounting business, you will need an organized office separate from the hubbub of the rest of your home. While this office does not need to be huge, you will be responsible for storing important tax receipts and records provided to you by your clients to prepare their taxes.

You shouldn't need to have clients come to your home, but if you can have an office space that allows for either a separate entrance or one very close to your office, that would be an advantage. Then you can have clients bringing you their materials rather than you running around collecting them.

Many clients will send you things, so you will need to plan on having courier services such as UPS, FedEx, and DHL stopping by regularly.

THINGS TO CONSIDER

If your work is mostly personal tax preparation, you work life will be intense from late January to April 15th. Plenty of people file for extensions, so you will have a more modest amount of work until August, the deadline for extensions. And a further extension can be had until October, so you will have another spurt of activity preparing returns in time for that extension. But the good news is that from mid October to the end of the year—when nice fall weather and the holidays kick in for most people—your workload will be relatively light.

HOW DO YOU WANT TO SPEND YOUR DAY?

With a tax preparation business, you will be spending your work time in your office chair. Most of your work will be computer work as well as weeding through receipts and other records, and some online searching for IRS publications and information.

WHAT YOU WILL NEED

For a business like this, you will want the usual comfortable desk setup with ergonomic furniture. Unless you have a computer system that is fairly new, purchase the latest desktop computer with printer and large-screen monitor. If you think you will be doing some of your work at your client's location, you may want to purchase a laptop instead of a desktop—but spring for a docking station that allows you to use a regular screen and keyboard when you are at your home office.

You should also plan to spend some money on tax preparation courses before you starting your business. The IRS offers courses for free.

MARKETING ANGLE

Don't plan to begin marketing to your potential clients until right after the new year—but that means January 2! No one wants to think about taxes during the holiday season. But the second the holiday season is over, you want to be seen and heard as the answer to their impending tax preparation woes. Try to get them on board before their W-2s are in their mailbox.

Another marketing angle will be to snag people when they are feeling overwhelmed with impending tax preparation. You may not get these clients until next year, or perhaps you can file an extension for them and help them out of their tax prep mess.

Whatever you do, present yourself as incredibly organized and unbelievably competent when it comes to tax preparation. You can increase your visibility and add to your credibility by writing a tax prep column in the local newspaper or online.

NICE TOUCH

If you do mostly small business tax preparation, consider offering a class during your slow times that teaches people thinking about starting a small business about the tax implications they will need to consider. Make the course inexpensive to take and learn about being a dynamic speaker. You just might end up with your students as clients!

EXPANSION POSSIBILITIES

The main way to expand in this business is to take on more clients. Start slow and make sure you are organized and accurate. You can even do this work part time before leaving a full-time position. This is not the kind of work where you are allowed to be overwhelmed.

WORDS TO KNOW

Capital Gains: The difference between what you paid for an investment and what you received when you sold that investment.

Corporation: A group of people who have organized to create a company to provides goods and/or services with the intention of making a profit.

RESOURCES

Working for a tax franchises like H&R Block is a great way to get your feet wet. Check out hrblock.com.

15 IMPORT/EXPORT SPECIALIST

Importing into and exporting out of the country is fraught with red tape and rules and regulations. Most business owners would love to expand their business to the rest of the world but either have no idea where to begin or get intimidated by the massive amounts of confusing paperwork. Get to know the ins and outs of the importing and exporting and you'll have a lucrative business on your hands.

If you don't already have work experience with importing and/or exporting, you will have a longer learning curve. But that doesn't mean you can't learn! The federal and state governments are always eager to encourage and support importing and exporting of goods and can be a great source of information and education in the import/export arena.

You can start by learning the basics and hosting educational sessions to teach others what they need to know to get started in import/export. That alone would probably gain you your first couple of clients. If you keep going with educational seminars and expand your reach to outside your immediate region, you could probably develop a sufficient and ongoing customer base very quickly, but be careful not to outpace your learning curve!

You will do best by starting slowly in this business. It is complicated and mistakes can be very costly to your clients. You can check with the chamber of commerce to see if there are any import/export seminars planned in your area to get you started.

HOW THIS BUSINESS IMPACTS YOUR HOME

You will need an office space in your home. This type of work will probably find you on the phone a lot, so it may be important to have an office space that is insulated from the daily hubbub of your household.

THINGS TO CONSIDER

This can be a frustrating business with mounds and mounds of paperwork. If you are impatient with government paperwork for the simplest of things, you don't want to be an import/export specialist—you may have pulled all your hair out before the end of the first week.

HOW DO YOU WANT TO SPEND YOUR DAY?

This is another occupation where you will spend most of your time in front of a computer. If you decide to do seminars, that would be a nice way to break up the computer time.

WHAT YOU WILL NEED

Besides a computer workstation, you will need other typical office peripherals, especially a fax machine. There is still a lot of paperwork that requires actual signatures. Sometimes a faxed version of the signature is fine and the fax machine can save time and money vs. having paperwork mailed or sent via overnight courier.

MARKETING ANGLE

Your marketing angle for this business is that if the only reason your potential customer is not in the import/export business is because they don't understand it, they can take that issue of their list. You understand it and you will get them dealing with the rest of the world, who would absolutely love their products.

UCH

Pick a country or two that you would like to do business with, or for whom several of your clients would be particularly well suited. If you know the language of those countries, market your language skills as an added bonus to working with you.

EXPANSION POSSIBILITIES

One way to expand in this service, especially if you are offering educational seminars, is to write a book about importing/exporting and sell it at your seminars and on your website.

Besides simply doing all the connecting and paperwork, you can also offer to be the export expert, bringing clients' products to other countries.

WORDS TO KNOW

F.O.B.: Free On Board: Refers to pricing, where the seller must deliver the goods on board the ship to the point named at the seller's expense.

Letter of Credit: A document issued by a bank at the buyer's request in favor of a seller, promising to pay an agreed amount of money upon receipt by the bank of certain documents within a specified time.

Rate of Exchange: Established and quoted for foreign currencies, the basis on which money of one country will be exchanged for that of another country.

RESOURCES

importexporthelp.com

exim.gov

business.gov/guides/import-export

FINANCIAL PLANNER 16

Financial planning has long been a hot business enterprise and will continue to be one. With the status of the social security system and the reluctance of companies to offer any significant retirement plans, Americans have now realized they are must take care of their own retirement. As a financial planner, you can be there to help people plan their financial future.

To start, you should go through the certification process so that you can label yourself a CFP (Certified Financial Planner). Your certificate shows that you have expertise and credibility, and this differentiation will help people choose you as their financial planner. Certification as a CFP involves six steps:

1. You must complete an education requirement by completing a CFP board registered education program and you must have a bachelor's degree (in any discipline). You may already fulfill the education requirement if you already have certain types of academic degrees or industry credentials, such as being a CPA, a CFA, a licensed attorney, or have a PhD in business or economics.

2. You must pass a Certification Examination. This exam tests your ability to apply your financial planning knowledge to client situations.

3. You must meet an Experience Requirement. At least three years of qualifying full-time work experience are required for certification.

4. You must pass a Candidate Fitness Standards and Background Check.

gree to abide by CFP Board's Code of Ethics and Professional Responsibility and Financial Planning Practice Standards. A background check will also be conducted.

5. You must pay certification fees.

6. You receive authorization to use the CPF logo, and CFP® and CERTIFIED FINANCIAL PLANNER™ designations.

For more information and details on all these steps, visit www.cfp.net/become/steps.asp.

HOW THIS BUSINESS IMPACTS YOUR HOME

For the financial planning business, you want a home office that is client-friendly, with a separate or almost separate entrance, a well-landscaped exterior, and particular attention to safety details in access areas. You may visit with your clients, but you will want an office base and access to the internet to conduct your research and provide people with accurate information and recommendations.

THINGS TO CONSIDER

Financial planning gives you a more evenly spaced workload than the other accounting-related businesses mentioned earlier, especially tax preparation. However, be ready for clients who are unprepared and who arrive at your door on April 13th to find out what investment they might make or other ways of reducing their tax burden. Clients will expect you to make up for their lack of planning.

HOW DO YOU WANT TO SPEND YOUR DAY?

Financial planning will require you to be sitting at a computer a lot of the time, especially given the wealth of information available on the internet.

However, this is one financial-related business where it is also important for you to get out and network with other financial experts on a regular basis. This will help you keep up to date on everything that is out there.

WHAT YOU WILL NEED

You will need a good computer system, a printer that can print a high number of high quality pages per minute, and access to lots of financial databases.

MARKETING ANGLE

The best marketing angle you can take with financial planning is to target an age group and/or income bracket. People in their late 20s who are just getting into careers and starting to think about home ownership and family will have very different financial planning needs and interests than those in their late 50s looking at starting a new career and how to have income beyond their main work-productive years. Everything about your service will need to speak to the age/income bracket you decide to focus on—the appearance of your marketing literature, the things you talk about, and the approach you take will all need to be tailored to the mindset of that age bracket.

NICE TOUCH

Clients like to think that their financial planners are thinking about them all the time. And you should be. Do a newsletter that keeps all your clients apprised of financial/retirement/investment news. Make it an e-newsletter with links so each client can easily click to get further information that might be of particular interest to them.

Plan to send your clients personal notes once or twice a month about things that are specific to their financial planning needs. And don't forget birthdays, weddings, deaths in the family—you will learn all of this about your clients since each significant event in a family may have financial implications.

EXPANSION POSSIBILITIES

One interesting and fun way to expand the financial planning business is to do seminars and workshops. You can reach more people and you can create a room full of prospective clients. If you write a book or create materials from your financial planning expertise, you can sell these to the seminar attendees.

WORDS TO KNOW

Estate: The overall planning of a person's wealth, including the preparation of a will and the planning of taxes after the individual's death.

Intestate: Having died without a will.

Revocable Trust: A trust in which provisions can be altered by the grantor. The grantor remains in control of the trust until after death when the property transfers to the beneficiary.

RESOURCES

Financial Planning magazine, financial-planning.com

Certified Financial Planner Board of Standards, cfp.net

TAXIDERMIST

17

Taxidermy is becoming a lost art. But if anatomy and physiology and nature intrigues you, taxidermy can be a fascinating homebased business. Today's world of taxidermy isn't exclusive to preserving real specimens. Taxidermy also refers to recreating a specimen using completely artificial materials.

Where would you find customers for taxidermy services? Hunters and fisherman are a huge customer base. According to www.taxidermy.net, a great example of artificial taxidermy is for catch-and-release fishermen. Anglers measure and take pictures of their catch before they release it back to the water. The taxidermist recreates the specimen into a wall mount, getting colors and size from the information and pictures provided from the fisherman.

Another source of clients for taxidermy are museums and other institutions. Even restaurants and hotels looking for a particular kind of décor are potential customers.

Taxidermy schools where you can learn the trade are located almost throughout the country, typically as courses over several weeks specializing in certain levels of expertise, from beginner to master's level. Many of these schools focus on helping students build a career and a taxidermy business. Most are hands-on and are therefore limited in size to a small number of students.

Like any enterprise, there are taxidermy conventions that you can attend and learn about the latest techniques and materials, as well as learn about ways to market your skills. These conventions take place throughout the country and all over the world, and often include competitions as well.

HOW THIS BUSINESS IMPACTS YOUR HOME

You will need a separate space for a taxidermy business. If you plan to work on real specimens, you will want a small shop outside of your home to make sure you don't offend the squeamish in your family. You will want an efficient workshop with good lighting and ventilation, and a large open table on which to work. If you already have an outbuilding you can easily convert, that's great. If not, a suitable sheds can be bought for well under $5,000, including construction.

THINGS TO CONSIDER

Taxidermists working with real animals need to be prepared to cut animals open and clean their inside structures. All taxidermists dealing with real animal specimens should be vaccinated against rabies and shouldn't work with wild animals found dead on the roadside, although this advice mostly falls on deaf ears when taxidermists are confronted with a rare specimen. In addition, most preservation chemicals are highly toxic, as are many glues. Keep materials out of reach of pets and small children.

HOW DO YOU WANT TO SPEND YOUR DAY?

Taxidermy is an art and you will be doing lots of close work inside a studio, much like other artists. You will need to know how to market your skills, so plan to attend conventions and network with other taxidermists.

WHAT YOU WILL NEED

This is one homebased business that doesn't rely on a computer, although having one would be handy for finding materials, searching for marketing opportunities and potential customers, and for handling your accounts and bookkeeping. You will need the work space mentioned above, and a small collection of tools such as tweezers, scissors, etc. If you plan to work with real specimens, you will want a freezer of appropriate size, which can often be bought used and very inexpensively.

MARKETING ANGLE

You can choose to market to museums and wildlife organizations for specimens, but you will need to get your skills up to museum-quality standards. You can also market your business to hunters and fishermen who would like trophies for their den or second home.

NICE TOUCH

Depending on whom you choose to market your taxidermy business to, you might consider donating to a wildlife organization—either annually or setting aside a portion of your profits or of each sale as a donation. There are tax benefits, of course, if you choose a legal nonprofit. Wildlife organizations often look to hunting and fishing communities for support in their efforts to preserve species and habitat.

EXPANSION POSSIBILITIES

As taxidermy is becoming a lost art, one expansion idea is to offer a class in preserving animal specimens.

WORDS TO KNOW

Mannikins: Forms used as the basis for sculpting the animal model.

Mount: A work of taxidermy; the creation of a lifelike, three-dimensional representation of an animal for permanent display. Some mounts contain natural parts of the animal; some (most notably saltwater fish) do not contain any parts of the animal at all.

RESOURCES

WASCO, Wildlife Artist Supply Company, taxidermy.com

Taxidermy.net has everything from a list of suppliers to lists of conventions, associations, and schools as well as a gallery of award-winning taxidermy projects.

eBAY ASSISTANT 18

Do you have items lurking around your household that you could sell on eBay? Perhaps a doll or baseball card collection you inherited but have little interest in? Or do you make something that you could sell in a regular eBay store? Perhaps you have some storage space where you could collect things and put them up for sale on eBay?

According to F/T & Research, eBay has 128 million members in the United States alone and over 173,000 stores hosted on their web site. This online auction company is currently valued in the billions of dollars. Selling goods on eBay has become big business for lots of people.

Collectibles represent the highest percentage of sales on eBay by far. Next comes clothing, shoes, and accessories, followed by entertainment, sports, home items, and jewelry and watches. Other popular categories include computers/electronics, toys/hobbies, books, pottery/glass, art, dolls/bears, antiques, business/industrial, coins, stamps, and musical instruments. According to F/T Research, people spend more time on eBay than any other site on the internet, and that amount increases around the holidays.

Selling on eBay is easy. Figure out your asking price and decide whether to auction it or put it in your eBay store. Then decide if you want a minimum bid and how long you want the auction to last. You will want to establish a PayPal account to use for transactions.

The eBay website provides all the information you need to know to get up and running with an eBay business. They are particularly interested in helping their users be successful and making sure that buyers get what they thought they were paying for—eBay's success depends on this insistence on customer service and quality of product and shipping. And as successful as eBay has been, they certainly have been making sure to keep both buyers and sellers happy.

HOW THIS BUSINESS IMPACTS YOUR HOME

The main impact you will find that selling on eBay has on your home is in storage needs, which is completely controllable depending on what you decide to sell and how much of it you want to sell. Otherwise, selling on eBay doesn't take much more space than a computer work area.

THINGS TO CONSIDER

Although it is a low-risk way of getting into business, selling regularly on eBay and having an eBay store takes some effort. Sellers need to create marketing text for their items, take digital photos or have print photos scanned and uploaded, keep tabs on the auction of their goods, update information, and pack and ship their goods in a timely manner.

HOW DO YOU WANT TO SPEND YOUR DAY?

If you get into selling on eBay in a big way, you will spend a lot of time in front of a computer screen. But at some point, you will need to get out of your chair and pack and ship things. Keep in mind that eBay buyers expect things to happen in a very timely fashion, so you need to keep your sales moving out the door. Pack things well and ship them right out. The eBay web site is set up for feedback on sellers—how well they packed things, how fast they shipped an item, whether items that people bought matched the description on the site and were of the quality the buyer was lead to believe. Your sales reputation will go up or down based on this feedback.

WHAT YOU WILL NEED

You need a computer work station with a printer. A digital camera is a must—it doesn't need to be fancy, but it must be capable of taking good pictures of the types of items you plan to sell. You might want a scanner and a fax machine. You will need to purchase some packing materials appropriate for shipping the types of items you are selling, and you need to create an efficient space in which to pack things up to be shipped out. You will also need some kind of storage to keep a certain amount of inventory on hand if you plan to make a substantial amount of money on eBay sales.

MARKETING ANGLE

Selling on eBay requires marketing just like any business. You will want to let people know you are selling items on eBay, especially if you are selling in a specific category. Learn about online marketing in general and use these skills to help sell your eBay items. Also, learn how to take photographs and write copy to present your products in an appealing way.

NICE TOUCH

The value of customer feedback for eBay sales cannot be underestimated. There are many things you can do to endear yourself to eBay buyers. For instance, without increasing your expenses drastically, always be sure to go above and beyond the minimum standard for safely shipping your products. While it's important to write marketing copy that makes your items sound enticing, always be completely honest—even point out negatives where they are relevant. Buyers will give you great feedback if they feel like they got what they thought they were buying and it arrived in excellent condition with apparent care paid to packaging.

EXPANSION POSSIBILITIES

There are a million ways to expand your business on eBay. If you start small and sell only an item or two here and there through the traditional eBay auctions, you can soon become hooked on stocking permanent items and selling through an eBay store. Check out the site—eBay itself will help you explore all the possibilities.

WORDS TO KNOW

Feedback: Customer comments and feedback play an important role in an eBay seller's status.

PayPal: A system tied into your checking or credit card account that allows money to be exchanged via email.

Shopping cart: An important system for selling products on the internet. Web sites contain a shopping cart function for buyers to select products and move them to their cart to purchase at the cyber-checkout.

RESOURCES

eBay.com

Entrepreneur Press, the publisher of this book, offers many titles on how to make money on eBay: entrepreneurpress.com.

BED AND BREAKFAST 19

A bed and breakfast might be a tough business to start and stay under the $5,000 startup focus of this book, but it can be done. The first thing that you have to own, of course, is a house that lends itself to renting out at least a room or two. If you want to create a retirement business with a B&B in your home, this is where you can start small and build up to that day when you are ready to take the bigger plunge.

Do you have a room that has its own bathroom and is private from the rest of the living space? Are you near attractions such as a tourist area, ski resort, large shopping complex, sports stadium, or venue for a large annual event? You can get your B&B feet wet marketing your one room to visitors to this one attraction. Or is your home in the country with spring peepers, summer crickets, and crisp fall nights that could give a city-dweller a weekend of peaceful living away from blaring horns and light pollution? Say you can rent the room for $150/night for Friday and Saturday nights 48 weeks/year—that's $14,400 in revenue!

Since breakfast is one of the Bs in B&B, you need to be able to offer it. If you don't have the setup for a formal dining area, perhaps there is a space in the bedroom for a drop-down table and you can bring a quaint breakfast of coffee, juice, homemade muffins, etc. to the door in a picnic basket.

If your space isn't perfect, don't just give up! Utilize what you have and create a unique experience. Tuck your one-room rental income away for a couple years and use it to renovate and create a second room. In five or six years, you could be ready for your full-fledged bed and breakfast with a customer base already in place!

Be sure that you comply with all regulations that the hospitality industry is subject to. Safety features, accessibility for people with disabilites, and truth in advertising regulations are critical to a service business.

HOW THIS BUSINESS IMPACTS YOUR HOME

Needless to say, this business impacts your home in a big way. If you start out slowly, as mentioned above, you will have your house to yourself all week but you will be sharing it with strangers most weekends. However, any bed and breakfast owner will tell you that most customers become regulars and many of them become friends, and you look welcome to their annual visit.

THINGS TO CONSIDER

Opening a bed and breakfast, especially via the one-room-slow-method, means you are opening your private home to strangers. Is your home set up so that your personal areas can be easily blocked off from the bed and breakfast rooms?

HOW DO YOU WANT TO SPEND YOUR DAY?

A bed and breakfast is a demanding business. If you can't hire help, you will be spending your time cooking breakfast, changing bedclothes and cleaning bathrooms, doing laundry and vacuuming, as well as marketing your business and taking reservations. Your day will be largely spent working on the business! If you start slow with one room while you are still gainfully employed elsewhere, you will need to spend evenings keeping your website up to date, trolling for customers, and making sure everything is in working order and doing repairs when things aren't.

WHAT YOU WILL NEED

You need a house that will accommodate a bed and breakfast setup. The rooms you offer these days need to be quiet and private—no longer do people accept sharing a bathroom down the hall. You will need to enjoy being friendly with strangers and having people at your home—they won't always realize that the backyard is off limits to guests or that they should park next to the barn, not up against the garage. This kind of business requires patience and a real customer-service attitude.

MARKETING ANGLE

If you live near a major attraction, focus on offering a combo package for accommodation and passes to the attraction. Perhaps you have a Buddhist tea room, you know some unusual craft like Zen flower arranging, or you can give guided tours of your historic downtown as a package deal. Your house itself may have historic appeal or unusual architecture. And if you enjoy being a host to pets as well as people, dog-friendly accommodations are a lucrative niche.

NICE TOUCH

There are hundreds of potential "nice touches" for the bed and breakfast world. Think about having a theme around your establishment. Maybe you have a small barn and could raise a few small animals such as chickens (fresh eggs!) and personable entertaining animals such as goats or alpacas. Or perhaps gardening is your thing and you could become known for a beautiful flower garden with a gazebo in the middle that guests could enjoy for breakfast or an evening cocktail. Use the natural features of your home to create a unique experience that your guests will tell their friends about.

EXPANSION POSSIBILITIES

Since you will need to start off very modestly in order to fit this startup into the "under $5,000" criteria of this book, expansion may mean nothing more than renovating another room to rent. Or you can start with just a room to rent in a home near a major attraction, but add passes and tours after that.

WORDS TO KNOW

Americans with Disabilities Act (ADA): a federal law concerned with making sure public buildings are accessible to disabled persons.

Homestay: A private home with one to four rooms for paying guests.

Soft opening: Testing a guest room for flaws with family members or friends before selling it to the public.

RESOURCES

Professional Association of Innkeepers International, paii.org

Bed & Breakfast Inns Online, bbonline.com

NOTARY PUBLIC/ JUSTICE OF THE PEACE

20

In most states in the U.S., a notary public is a state officer who is authorized to witness and attest to the legalities of certain documents by signature and stamping a seal. Most states require that you pass an exam and a background check. Notaries have no authority to offer legal advice or act as a lawyer in any way. It costs very little to become a notary and your income from notary work is negligible.

A justice of the peace typically performs wedding ceremonies. States have varying rules and procedures for becoming a JP and performing services. For instance, in the commonwealth of Massachusetts, a JP is appointed by the Governor and serves a seven-year term. Applications are available through the Secretary of State's office and only one JP is allowed for every 5000 residents in a town or city.

Becoming a JP and/or Notary Public does not cost much money. And it is not a big moneymaking venture! Many states set the fees you can charge for JP services, which, in Massachusetts, are currently $75 for a wedding ceremony in the town of the JPs jurisdiction and $125 for other locations. JPs can add additional fees, and often do, including travel and hourly rates for additional meetings such as rehearsals, other prep time, and any special requests. Always be upfront with clients about all of the fees you charge.

This is a homebased business that is leisurely and one that can make a nice side business for someone in retirement or who has other commitments.

HOW THIS BUSINESS IMPACTS YOUR HOME

People wishing for notary public services may call you and want to come to your home with the papers they wish to have notarized. You will want to have an organized desk or table where they can sit to witness their signatures and sign and notarize their documents. And they will probably write you out a check. Having a neat place with your notary seal handy will make the visit quicker and you will look efficient and organized.

JP work is most likely to happen outside your home. Most people wishing to get married using a justice of the peace will ask that you marry them in the place of their choice. Depending on your state's laws, you can marry people in the town of your jurisdiction or in the town of their choice. If their local JP isn't available on their preferred date, the JP will give them a list of other JPs they can check with—if you network with your fellow JPs, that list will include you.

THINGS TO CONSIDER

Decide how many weddings you are willing to do in a month's time. The majority of weddings happen on a weekend but you can get requests for any time of the week. Don't feel like you have to do every wedding request that comes your way.

If you want to line up a lot of ceremonies, be sure to get your name on lists with wedding-related services, such as florists, wedding gown shops, tuxedo and limo rentals, etc.

HOW DO YOU WANT TO SPEND YOUR DAY?

You can make this a fairly low-impact business. Typically your notary work will come unexpectedly, while JP work can be a little more planned.

WHAT YOU WILL NEED

Beyond the application fee, you will need to purchase the embosser or ink stamp for your work as a notary public.

For JP, you will need to promote your wedding officiant services. You can make this service a small or large as you want, offering special packages or themed ceremonies serving much like a wedding consultant! Or you can simply show up for the service and do whatever the person-in-charge tells you to do, and then leave.

You might even want to create a space in your home or yard specifically for conducting weddings. Do you have a gazebo? That's a lovely wedding spot!

Weddings conducted by JPs are typically small in size, so you won't need an enormous space to be suitable for a wedding. You can either have the other accoutrements on hand (chairs for guests, a table for a guest book, a music source, etc.) or let the wedding party take care of all of that and you just provide the venue and the legal representation. How deeply you want to get into it is up to you and your available space.

MARKETING ANGLE

As a JP, you can offer not only a venue, but a venue that has some sort of centerpiece such as a gazebo or flower garden or lakeside arbor. Put an image of that feature on all your marketing materials.

NICE TOUCH

A simple nice touch is to have a small gift that you offer the wedding couple, such as a book of thoughtful sayings or a picture frame for one of their wedding photos. If you have a digital camera, you can have a family member take a few pictures of the ceremony, print them out on a portable photo printer, and pop that picture into a frame as an immediate gift.

EXPANSION POSSIBILITIES

If you start out just officiating ceremonies, you can expand by adding some of the wedding planning, such as creating a venue to host your ceremonies.

WORDS TO KNOW

Adjudicate: To come to a judicial decision.

Inquests: A judicial or official inquiry or examination, particularly in front of a jury.

Jurisdiction: The area in which the JP or notary's legal authority covers.

RESOURCES

Look on your state's official website for justice of the peace information.

Massachusetts Justice of the Peace Association, mjpa.org

WEBSITE DEVELOPER 21

The internet is an integral part of today's business world. Any business of any size must have a website to be competitive. Even if the business owner decides not to actually conduct sales on the website, today's potential customers expect to be able to compare businesses, what they offer in both products and services, and simply get an overall sense of the company by sitting at home in front of their computer and calling up the company's website.

Large corporations can afford to have an onsite Information Technology person. Medium-sized corporations may not have enough work or resources to keep an on-staff IT person; they often hire out this kind of work to a freelancer or outside company who specializes in computer technology for business applications. And small businesses are looking for another small business to take care of their computer needs. This often specifically means website development and maintenance, and this is where you come in.

The technical side of website design is not especially difficult. Many courses exist (many of which, logically, are offered online) where you can learn the language of website creation and can learn about the details, like how to set up shopping cart systems, security concerns, etc.

One of the most important and less concrete things you will need to learn is about design issues surrounding websites. If visitors click out of the website as fast as they click into it, your web-designing business will be short-lived. Web design includes learning the answers to these questions:

- What makes a visitor stay at a website?

- What are the good elements of a home page?

- What design features influence efficient use of a website?

- What features do today's web visitors expect?

You will, of course, need to learn about each company you design for. What makes them unique in their chosen industry? What are their company values? What is the atmosphere of the company that you need to reflect in the website design—is it wild and contemporary, meaning brilliant colors and fun graphics are important? Or will more classic colors like black, navy blue, and/or maroon be more appropriate?

All of this is the fun stuff of website design—pulling together the information you need to create the most appropriate and user-friendly site for the company who hired you.

HOW THIS BUSINESS IMPACTS YOUR HOME

This business should have a low impact on your home. You will need space for a good computer system and work station, as well as privacy for sometimes lengthy phone conversations. But you will do most of your non-computer work outside the home, at the offices of your clients.

THINGS TO CONSIDER

You will absolutely spend most of your work time with this business sitting in front of a computer. However, as has been mentioned several times already, when you work for yourself at home, there is no one telling you that you can't get up out of your chair and get a snack, walk the dog, jog in the park, take your kids to the playground after school, or run a few errands any time you need to or feel the need to get up and move around.

HOW DO YOU WANT TO SPEND YOUR DAY?

If you don't mind spending your day steeped in the latest technology and interacting mostly with a computer, you can enjoy this creative business.

WHAT YOU WILL NEED

You will need a better-than-average computer work station with a large-screen monitor and high-speed internet access. Plan to purchase web design software as well as photo manipulation software. You should have a phone system that has either a speaker phone or other hands-free access so you can work on your computer and talk at the same time.

You need to take some web site design classes to make sure you know all the latest whiz-bangs available for websites. Unless you have an art or publishing background or degree, you should also consider a general design class and a publishing-related design class that will teach you about color use and typography. Website design classes will cover some of this as well. These things will ensure you are competitive in today's web design world.

MARKETING ANGLE

If you feel you can produce only a certain style of website, don't try to be something you are not—go with it, and do it the very best you can. There are loads of new website development customers almost every day so there will be plenty who your style appeals to. Make sure all your marketing materials—including your own website!—showcase that style.

NICE TOUCH

Websites need to be constantly updated. Offer a certain amount of updating and changes for free within the first month or two of the website design going live—this will relieve the pressure on the company that in order to get their money's worth they need to get everything right the first time around. This also gets them in the mindset that a website is somewhat fluid. Then include a fee schedule for ongoing updates, so you can keep a certain amount of income generating from an established client. Send them monthly mini e-newsletters that educate them on new website design issues and features and encourage them to hire you to do ongoing work on their site.

EXPANSION POSSIBILITIES

You can go beyond simple website design and offer hosting and updating services. Start an e-newsletter that offers tips on how to create a great website, the latest trends in website design, and the latest in security features. Expand your offering by becoming a total website expert.

WORDS TO KNOW

Home Page: The page on a website that the browser opens to and provides an overview of the company or organization that owns the site.

HTML: Acronym of Hypertext Markup Language, the computer language that is used to create websites.

Meta tags: Code inserted into your HTML code that help search engines understand the content of your site.

RESOURCES

websitepros.com

htmlcodetutorial.com

FREELANCE GRAPHIC DESIGNER

22

Designing print media for companies is a fun, interesting, and potentially lucrative business. Despite the proliferation of the internet, print media is here to stay for the foreseeable future! Fliers, newsletters, magazines, information sheets, letters, and advertisements are just a few of the types of print media that business hire freelancers to create for them.

However, graphic design is not relegated only to print media. Websites and online advertising need graphic design services as well. Web design will require a somewhat different mindset, but you still use the same thinking when it comes to page composition and what people respond to. However, the use of animation and how color works on the screen is different compared to print materials.

Even if your expertise is only in design, offer the works for potential clients, including the editorial creation and the printing and even mailing of the final piece. You can line up regular freelancers for those parts of the job you can't do, giving you the ability to offer full-service media creation while not having to have all of this expertise yourself or have all of these people who do on staff.

To be successful at graphic design, you must be sure to stay up to date on design trends. If you focus on designing for a certain industry, read their trade magazines and look at the industry's websites, and keep abreast of general design trends as well.

HOW THIS BUSINESS IMPACTS YOUR HOME

You will also need an area in your house that allows you to spread your work out—and it should be out of the way of general home traffic so you can keep work spread out while you are in the middle of a project. You should be able to visit most clients or do most of your client interaction via phone or email, so you don't have to worry about clients coming to your home. You will need to keep your driveway clear if you live in the snowbelt, keep the kids' toys out of the driveway, and the dogs at bay, since you will probably get several courier deliveries a week. You can send much of your work via email if your clients have the computer capabilities or an FTP site to accept large files, but you'll more likely be burning large graphics to DVDs and shipping them out.

THINGS TO CONSIDER

This is another one of those businesses where you will spend much of your time sitting at a computer. Be sure to get ergonomic equipment and office furniture to take good care of your back and avoid injuries like carpal tunnel syndrome.

HOW DO YOU WANT TO SPEND YOUR DAY?

You will be working in front of a computer and sitting inside most of the time. Instead of faced with print all day, you will be able to enjoy looking at more graphics and varying material.

WHAT YOU WILL NEED

You will need a better-than-average computer system with lots of memory, loaded with professional-grade graphics software. You'll need a large-screen monitor, a scanner, a DVD burner, and a reliable backup drive, plus a high-speed internet connection. As mentioned earlier, you will need a spacious work station and decent office furniture that doesn't stress your back and cause problems with the repetitive motion inherent in computer work.

MARKETING ANGLE

One way to target your marketing in this wide-open field is to pick a type of customer and market directly to them. Perhaps there is a field or industry you have prior experience with. Perhaps your area is known for a certain industry (High Point, NC, for furniture, Detroit for cars, for example) that you can target. Or perhaps there is an industry you would like to know more about—sometimes the best designs can come from a fresh eye. Promote that.

NICE TOUCH

Line up two or three people who can provide proofreading services for any print piece you create, whether you were responsible for the editorial or not. Letting customers know you have this quality-control service helps relieve them of the burden of being concerned about the accuracy of the final piece. Of course, they need to be responsible for the accuracy of the information and any numbers they provide, but at least their credibility is not impacted by misspelled, missing, or misused words.

EXPANSION POSSIBILITIES

You can start slow by targeting a specific industry and then add industries to your repertoire.

WORDS TO KNOW

Dummy: A mockup of design work that allows the customer to decide whether the design works for what they want before the designer creates and prints the final design.

Kerning: Adjusting the space between letters.

Saturation: The color intensity of an image.

RESOURCES

graphicdesign.about.com

graphicdesign.com

RUG CLEANING

23

People have little enough time these days to do simple housecleaning. They often leave the big jobs—like rug cleaning—to professionals. You will want to be able to do both onsite cleaning and have a setup to be able to clean area rugs at your own establishment.

As with any business, you need to have a base of operations that consists mostly of a computer to keep track of appointments and do billing. Your customers will come from word-of-mouth advertising by satisfied clients, but as with any business, you will want to create (or have someone create for you) a simple website that tells about your service and probably includes a price list.

You will need to learn how to work with all kinds of carpet fabrics from synthetic to wool carpets. Decide whether or not you will take on valuable antique carpets and family heirlooms; if so, you will want to get specialized training in how to handle these carpets and the specialized ways of cleaning them. Learn how to get tough stains and odors out of carpets—such as dog and cat odors—and your services will be in great demand.

HOW THIS BUSINESS IMPACTS YOUR HOME

Unless you stick strictly to onsite cleaning, some people will want to drop carpets off at your home. If you are doing in-home cleaning, you will want to be able to take over a bay in the garage or have some other open facility with a cement floor and preferably a drain. If you do not have an existing space that would make an appropriate rug cleaning work space but have the room, creating a cement pad of approximately 16' X 16' to accommodate most area rugs, is not that difficult or expensive. In fact, the site work of preparing the base before the concrete is poured can be the most expensive part. Put the pad some place where you might eventually want to create a small garage or otherwise plan to some day make a covered building. In the meantime, you can erect a portable "instant" garage over all or part of the cement pad to have both covered and open space to hose down, clean, air out, and dry carpets.

Of course, no matter how you do it, you need to have a way to lock up valuable carpets while they are in your possession. Again, an extra bay in the garage that may not be appropriate for cleaning carpets might still be able to be used to store carpets until their owners retrieve them. If you plan to pick up and deliver carpets in the van you lease for the business, you can use your vehicle for secure storage, with the exception of extra large carpets that may not fit in the vehicle and need to be stored elsewhere until delivered.

Another option is to rent a storage unit, which have cropped up everywhere and are reasonably priced and good to use for equipment and supply storage while building up a business.

THINGS TO CONSIDER

Professional cleaning of almost anything involves working with a certain amount of chemicals. While they may not be toxic, many of them are and most are at least abrasive. You need to decide if you want to spend your time working with these kinds of products. You can certainly learn to minimize your contact. Plus, you can make sure you bring along fans to move fumes out the door at your onsite jobs, and install a whole-house type fan in your workspace at home.

There will be some heavy lifting involved with carpet cleaning—the cleaning machines can be quite heavy and large area carpets themselves are on the heavy side. Learn how to lift with your knees to spare your back! You will also learn tricks of the trade, like using a long two-by-four to move a rolled up carpet around more easily.

HOW DO YOU WANT TO SPEND YOUR DAY?

Carpet cleaning is a physically demanding job. You are on your feet most of the time and, as mentioned earlier, you need the strength to do some heavy lifting. When you aren't doing the physical labor of cleaning carpets, you will be spending your time driving from site to site for your jobs.

WHAT YOU WILL NEED

You will need a portable carpet cleaning machine to do the onsite jobs, and a vehicle that is appropriate to transport it—preferably a van or SUV (many SUVs allow you to remove the back row of seats, leaving a nice compromise between a truck and a van). Also, as mentioned above, if you do some of your work at your home, you will need a space; either an empty bay in the garage or a cement pad at the end of the driveway, on which you could erect a portable instant storage area.

MARKETING ANGLE

Carpet cleaning can be a daunting task. Market to homeowners the ease of which carpets can be cleaned using your services, and to businesses how important clean carpets are to their overall appearance.

NICE TOUCH

Consider using natural cleaning products. In an increasingly green business environment, this could be a selling point for your carpet cleaning services ("safe for pets and children") and might distinguish you from other carpet cleaning services in your area. It's also healthier for you in the long run.

EXPANSION POSSIBILITIES

If you start out just doing carpet cleaning on the road, consider expanding by creating a venue at your home where you can clean up to room-sized carpets; that way, the homeowner doesn't have to be home while you work.

WORDS TO KNOW

Antimicrobial: A chemical that prevents the growth of bacteria, mold, and mildew, and the destruction they do to carpet fibers.

Neutral Cleaner: A cleaning product having a pH of 7, which is considered neutral, i.e., neither acid nor base.

Pile lifter: A type of heavy duty vacuum cleaner that re-erects the pile in a carpet.

RESOURCES

Carpet-cleaning.net

Cleaning-carpet-tips.com

PROPERTY MANAGEMENT 24

Do you enjoy home care and home repair? Do you understand the fundamentals of how a home works? Do you know how to hire the right professionals—plumbers, electricians, and landscapers—to get things done? You might be perfect for the property management business.

In order to undertake this type of business, you will need to live in an area where there are homes that are not lived in by their owners. This could be seasonal homes lakeside or oceanfront homes or it could be rental properties in multi-unit complexes.

Your job, in the case of rental units, will be to make sure the property is running smoothly. For seasonal properties, you will most likely spend your management time making sure the property is ready for seasonal visits and well maintained when no one is around. If the owners go away for six weeks in the winter, the property manager makes regular checks on the property to make sure the pipes aren't leaking, that the furnace is running and has fuel if the owners chose to keep the heating system on, any newspapers or mail are not left cluttering up the mailbox area, the security system is on and functioning, and (in northern climates) the driveway is plowed after snowstorms, You will be the contact number if the security system operator needs to contact someone about a breach in security.

Property management is a big job but it has the potential for big income if you become good at it and learn the ins and outs of making everything go smoothly.

HOW THIS BUSINESS IMPACTS YOUR HOME

This business shouldn't have much impact on your home beyond requiring space for the usual computer setup—which can be as simple as a laptop with a printer in the corner of the living room. You will want a phone system, although with this kind of on-the-road work it may be best to have a cellular phone to conduct all your business.

THINGS TO CONSIDER

You will be essentially on call at all hours. How much that impacts your life depends on how many and what kind of clients you bring in. If you are the point person for a 25-unit rental complex, you may get a lot of calls. On the other hand, as property manager, you don't have to be the day-to-day point person. The owner can still hire a building supervisor who calls you when there is something she or he can't handle.

HOW DO YOU WANT TO SPEND YOUR DAY?

This can be very hectic work. If you like your day to be a fairly predictable and peaceful, you might consider different work.

WHAT YOU WILL NEED

The main thing you need is a reputation for being honest and reliable. No one will hire you to do property management unless you have references saying you can remain cool in crisis and are impeccably honest.

You will need a vehicle, preferably one that can hold tools in case you need to do minor repairs. You need a cell phone and a computer. Other than that, there is not much in the way of overhead expenses.

MARKETING ANGLE

One of the best marketing angles you can have as a property manager is proof of being trustworthy—have testimonials that pay tribute to how you are always looking out for the property owner's best interests. Be fair with everyone and avoid a reputation of being difficult to deal with.

NICE TOUCH

If you make your property management focus taking care of people's seasonal homes during the off season, create a newsletter template and once a month send news about their home-away-from-home. Inform them about any town-related tidbits that are decided during elections, issues with the road they live on, or any zoning decisions that impact the area in which their home is located. When it gets close to their arrival, let them know about upcoming events they might want to attend.

EXPANSION POSSIBILITIES

The expansion with property management is to take on larger clients with several properties to manage. However, you don't want to put all your eggs in one basket so be sure to have a few different clients in case one sells out or goes broke. You can also expand by increasing the services you offer.

WORDS TO KNOW

Onsite property manager: A manager that lives on the property.

Escalation clause: A clause contained in a lease that allows the rent to increase when a certain event occurs.

Fair Housing Laws: Laws that prevent housing discrimination based on race, color, national origin, religion, sex, familial status, or disability.

RESOURCES

bonding insurance, cbic.com

National Property Management Association, npma.org

Almost everyone can take a walk through their home and collect several boxes of stuff that they no longer want. Why not get some of your money back to buy things you need?

Kitchen utensils, knickknacks, computer accessories, office supplies, clothing, craft supplies, that odd piece of pottery you got for a wedding present 15 years ago that you've never used, you name it—people love to spend weekends rummaging through tables full of other people's unwanted items, looking for treasures.

Make sure to put prices on your items. If you don't want to put tags or stickers on a bunch of small stuff, group them in boxes or on tables by price. Or just stick a small colored dot on them and scatter them around—anything with a blue dot is fifty cents, red is a quarter, etc. Don't make people make you an offer unless you have something big and don't want to limit it to a price. That telescope that's been sitting in the back bedroom for ten years might have been worth $200 new, but you might want to let someone make you an offer for what they can afford for it. But even then, put a tag on it that says. "Bought new for $200. Make offer." If you don't, people will often just walk away instead of inquiring. You want everyone to walk away having purchased something!

Make sure to change your layout and put new stuff out for sale often. You want people to come back time and again to see what's new. You don't even have to have that much new stuff to make things look new. Just moving an item from a table to the top of a bookshelf might get it noticed, even though the item has been in your inventory since you first started having sales.

If you don't have enough stuff to keep having sales regularly, go find it! This is easier if you conduct your sales just once a month. Ask all your friends and relatives if they have stuff you can add to your sale. Either offer them an overall price or sticker their items with a color that indicates what is theirs; you can pay them a percentage of the sale.

HOW THIS BUSINESS IMPACTS YOUR HOME

A flea market business at your home can have significant impact. You will need to carve out a space to have your sale. And you will need to be there, of course. If you have a spouse or children, you can recruit them to help with the sale. A little financial incentive always helps!

THINGS TO CONSIDER

Having a "yard sale" or "tag sale" (the lingo changes in different parts of the country) one or two weekends a year is one thing. Having one every weekend is quite another. You will want to check zoning regulations for your neighborhood to find out exactly how you can operate. Perhaps it's OK to have ten yard sales a year. Do you want to be open ten weekends in a row for ten weeks? Or do you want to be open every other weekend for five months? Or perhaps, depending on your climate, the first weekend of every month for ten months of the year?

HOW DO YOU WANT TO SPEND YOUR DAY?

While you are open for business, you need to be at home. This is not a business you can conduct when you happen to be home; you need to come up with some regular hours and be there when you say you will be. The most common time for people to be out and about and willing to stop to browse a flea market will be weekends, particularly all day Saturday and Sunday. So if you actually want to have substantial sales, you will need to plan to conduct all of your business on weekends.

WHAT YOU WILL NEED

You need a place to conduct your sale. No matter where you have it, you need tables, chairs, clothes racks, boxes, bookshelves, and other types of display furniture for your items to be visible.

If your area is zoned so that you can have your sale all the time, any time, you will probably want to set up in the garage or an outbuilding. That way, you can always be under cover and you don't have to move everything in and out every time you have your sale. If you are only going to have a flea market once a month, it is easy enough to set up each time.

Plan to have some change on hand. Be sure you have a calculator, a few pens, and a pad of paper, just in case someone wants directions or you want to make a list of things people seem to be looking for in particular. Have a comfortable chair, some reading material, even a laptop for the down times.

You will need a sign at the end of the driveway to indicate to passersby that you are having a sale. You'll want to have some signage directing people where to park, if it isn't obvious.

If your sale gets popular enough, you might want to rent a port-a-john just for one weekend a month, although people rarely expect that.

MARKETING ANGLE

One way to market your flea market business is to become known for a specific kind of item. If you sell a lot of collectibles, furniture, or dishware, people interested in buying those items will spread the word.

NICE TOUCH

Add a "locally made" section to your sale. You'd be amazed what your friends, family, and neighbors make. It adds a nice touch to your sale. You can either offer these things each time you have your sale, or have a different theme each month, such as baked goods, fiber crafts, winter wear, nature items, fresh produce, or wood crafts.

EXPANSION POSSIBILITIES

How much can you expand with a homebased flea market will depend a lot on the zoning for "tag sales," "yard sales," or "flea markets" in your area. If you can only sell once/month, you might want to consider upgrading the items that you do sell. Instead of selling dishware, sell used furniture. Instead of selling furniture, sell antiques. If your flea market specialty is books, also sell bookcases to add a higher ticket item to your offerings.

WORDS TO KNOW

Variance: When a property owner wants to do something on their property that is not allowed by zoning, the property owner needs to apply to the town for a variance to the rule.

Zoning restrictions: The rules and regulations established by a town that delineate how property in certain areas can be used. For example, your road or neighborhood may have zoning regulations that permit homeowners to have no more than one yard sale per month.

RESOURCES

Flea market merchandise, wholesalenc.com

Aaafleamarketsupply.com

26 DOG BREEDER

Pets are phenomenally popular. In the U.S., 39 percent of U.S. households have a dog as a pet; 25 percent of those have two dogs, totaling 74.8 million dogs (according to recent statistics conducted by The Humane Society of the United States). Many people are willing to go to animal shelters and adopt a dog that needs a home. Many others are looking for a specific breed; purebred dogs are more popular than ever and they are commanding large sums of money.

However, dog breeding is a complicated business. Consumers are more savvy than ever before, and that includes what they expect from pet purchases. You will need to establish yourself as a conscientious breeder who cares about the health and welfare of the animals you bring into the world. This can be expensive, and is the reason purebred dogs can be sold for higher prices.

If you are considering breeding dogs as a business, you most likely already like dogs. But breeding can bring your dog life to a whole new level. Dogs can be a lot of work just as pets; breeding dogs is a whole lot more work.

Before finding the appropriate mate for your female dog, you need to make sure she is in impeccable physical condition for her mothering responsibilities. You need to learn about nutrition both during pregnancy and after whelping. You need to be sure you have an adequate and safe place for her to have her puppies and what to do if something goes wrong. And you need to know all about raising puppies from the time they are born to the time they are ready to go to their new homes. And all of that doesn't cover marketing your puppies to sell them!

You could decide to go into the other aspect of the dog breeding business, and raise a male dog that you use as a stud. You would then charge breeders to breed their females to your male. This is not as easy as it may seem. In order for your male dog to command any kind of worthwhile stud fee, you need to get him out starting at a young age to earn points in competition—this could be breed shows, agility competitions, or whatever, depending on the dog's abilities and your interest. But your stud will have to have been incredibly well bred himself and earn his name in the world before you can ask high prices for breeding fees. And having an intact male dog can be much more complicated than a female—they have the urge to roam in search of females and if you aren't careful with behavior issues, male dogs can be aggressive and territorial. Of course, a lot depends on the individual but these are things to consider. On the positive side, keeping a male dog at stud is a lot less work than raising and selling puppies!

In order to be a reputable breeder, it is imperative that you become known within your veterinary community—these are the people who will recommend your breeding program and your puppies to their clients who are looking for the breed of dog you are selling. Veterinarians don't tend to say negative things about their clients; they simply will not recommend you and will recommend another breeder if a client asks about the type of dogs you are breeding.

HOW THIS BUSINESS IMPACTS YOUR HOME

Having puppies in your home is a whole lot of fun as well as a whole lot of chaos! It is best if your breeding kennel is apart from your main house, even if it is just in a warm-in-winter/cool-in-summer extension like a renovated garage, shed, or mudroom with an attached, safe, outdoor kennel.

THINGS TO CONSIDER

Many breeds have genetic propensities like certain cancers, eye problems, and hip dysplasia. Learn everything you can about the breed you are considering. Not only do you want to avoid breeds that have serious medical problems, but you want your customers to know that you understand the breed inside and out. With that in mind, choose breeding dogs whose pedigree is clear of any genetic health problems.

Breeding animals is serious business; it should be done responsibly and with the same care and compassion you have for your own personal pets. Having a reputation for bringing less-than-high-quality puppies into the world will ruin your business fast. Promote responsible pet ownership by being a responsible breeder.

HOW DO YOU WANT TO SPEND YOUR DAY?

Depending on how many breeding females you decide to have, you may think dog breeding will entail a lot of downtime—female dogs (called "bitches") come into heat and are able to be bred only twice a year. If you really want your puppies to be in demand and your dogs to command high prices, you will want them to have won awards in shows and competitions. The thinking in animal competition is that if the bitch or the dog placed high in competitions, their offspring have a greater chance of also being winners.

You can either do this yourself—which means spending a lot of time on the road getting to the various competitions, grooming your dog, and learning how to handle the dog in a show. Or you can hire someone to do all that for you—which means you need to be very serious about earning money back from that dog.

WHAT YOU WILL NEED

To keep a dog breeding business under the $5,000 limit, you will need to start off slowly. You can buy a breeding-age "proven" animal and pay a couple thousand dollars for her, or you can purchase a puppy with unknown breeding capabilities from a reputable breeder for less. Be aware she will need to be at least two years old before you breed her. You need to be sure to tell a breeder from whom you buy a puppy that you will be breeding the dog. Be aware that they keep competitors at bay by charging more for the pup that is intended to be part of a breeding program. And they make anyone else sign papers saying they will not breed the dog, and in fact, will get the pup neutered or spayed.

You will need a safe place for your dog to play and hang out. You want your kennel area to be clean and attractive, not just for the dog's health but also to be appropriate for people to come and view the puppies.

For the puppy stage, you will want a safe and comfortable whelping area for the female to have her puppies. As the puppies grow older, they will be extremely active—if you decide on a medium-sized breed like Labrador Retrievers whose litters are commonly eight to ten pups, you will need a fairly large space for those puppies to spend their first months.

Plan to spend several hundred dollars preparing the female for breeding, making sure she is appropriately vaccinated for your area, that her reproductive system is examined, and that any breed-specific issues are investigated to ensure she has no genetic issues that she may pass along to her pups.

MARKETING ANGLE

With puppy mills more prevalent than ever, market your dogs as literally home grown. Promote that they already know about living in a home environment and have heard the sound of the vacuum cleaner, interacted with children and other dogs, and begun to learn about how to behave around furniture and how to act appropriately at meal times. But make sure you have trained your puppies for all of these first!

NICE TOUCH

Include some pictures on your website and any print media you create that shows your dogs in a family situation. While you want to also include the ribbon-winning shots, most people do not buy dogs for competition; most buy dogs for pets. They will be enticed to buy your dogs after seeing pictures of you cuddling with them or them sleeping on the family sofa with your young child, etc.

EXPANSION POSSIBILITIES

If you find you like breeding and selling purebred dogs, you can start with one breed and move into another. Or, since you already have the beginnings of a kennel arrangement, you could offer boarding or "doggie daycare," another aspect of dog ownership that has grown in popularity. You could also branch out into grooming or pet food sales.

WORDS TO KNOW

Doggie daycare: A popular type of short-term boarding—usually for all or part of a work day—for dogs. They are usually allowed a period of supervised play time.

Genetics: The makeup of an animal's cells that tell what the animal will look like and to what kind of diseases it may be predisposed.

Puppy mill: A term used for a business that keeps large numbers of animals and breeds them constantly, warehousing as many puppies as possible to sell to pet shops and other outlets for dogs.

Whelping: The actual birth of the puppies.

RESOURCES

dogbreedinginformation.net

American Kennel Club, akc.org

27 CHRISTMAS TREE SALES

This seasonal business can be a nice income-generator just when you need a little extra cash for the holiday gift-buying season. In the U.S., 28 million U.S. households purchased a real tree in 2006 for their Christmas decorating, according to the National Christmas Tree Association, with 63 percent of those tree purchases being from a tree farm or either a for-profit or nonprofit retail lot. It's worth noting that 2006 was the first year statistics were shown for online sales of Christmas trees, with 4 percent of households buying their tree off the internet.

The 2006 retail value of those trees sold was $1.2 billion, with real trees selling for an average of $40-50 each.

If you want to start a Christmas tree farm, you need to plan ahead. It takes approximately seven years for a Balsam fir—perhaps the most traditional Christmas tree—to grow from a small sapling to a five- to six-foot tree, the size expected for those brought into the house to be decorated. Of course, such an undertaking involves a few acres of land. Even if you live in a city or suburb, you certainly can consider purchasing land in the country and growing trees on it. If you already own a plot of land that makes sense to clear (or, better yet, is already clear), growing your own trees to sell will be easier.

You need to visit your tree farm a few weekends per year; most trees don't grow naturally into that triangular shape, and need to be pruned annually and encouraged to take the shape people have come to expect from a Christmas tree.

If you do decide to grow your own trees to sell, you have a couple of different options for selling them. Becoming a wholesaler and selling your trees to someone else for them to mark up in price and sell to consumers will bring you the least amount of revenue—and you would need a considerable size tree farm to make this a worthwhile venture. Selling your trees yourself is the best option.

You can decide to have what is typically known as a "choose -and-harvest" operation. Much like a "pick your own" fruit or vegetable farm, the consumer comes to the property, wanders around looking at trees, picks the one they want, and harvests it or tags it and you harvest it for them. Visitors to this type of tree farm expect a full experience—you'll want to offer light refreshments like hot mulled cider and donuts/cookies, along with a horsedrawn sleigh or wagon (hire someone to do this for you!) to tote visitors and their trees, a firepit, etc. Visits from Santa Claus are also a nice touch.

The other option—certainly simpler and falling within the $5,000 parameter—is to buy your trees from a wholesaler and sell them either in your yard or in a vacant lot that you rent from Thanksgiving to Christmas. Tree wholesalers throughout the country can be located on a map on the National Christmas Tree Association's website. Plan to also sell wreaths, kissing balls, and other Christmas decorating-related items.

HOW THIS BUSINESS IMPACTS YOUR HOME

If you conduct your sales away from your home, the impact on your home is minimal, although the impact on your home life can be considerable since you will be gone much of the time between Thanksgiving and Christmas. For an already busy time of year, this can make doing sales from home a lot more logical.

THINGS TO CONSIDER

This can be a great business for the family teenager to operate. Mom and Dad may have to front the money for the trees for the first couple years, but if you help your teen figure out how much to set aside each year for next year's tree purchase, it can quickly get to the point where the business revenue takes care of its own purchases.

Another thing to consider is that it can be difficult to determine how many trees to have available. You would prefer to run out of trees than have dozens hanging around on December 25th. That said, plan in advance how to dispose of your excess trees once Christmas comes.

HOW DO YOU WANT TO SPEND YOUR DAY?

Selling trees requires you to be outdoors just as the northern climates are turning cold. Often you will need to be outdoors in the evening hours because this is when your working customers will shop for their trees. And for five to six weeks, your weekends will be consumed with tree sales as well.

WHAT YOU WILL NEED

You will need a source of trees, whether you grow your own or buy from a wholesaler. You will need plenty of warm clothes, and dress in layers— if sales get hopping, you will warm up fast! You need some way to stand the trees up—and sturdy A-frame type arrangement that the trees can lean against is sufficient. Plan to have tags that clear indicate the price of the tree. If it's raining or snowing, you will want some kind of shelter, even if it is just a canopy, in order to get out of the elements while it's not busy. You will need some amount of change, although it's best to price your trees in increments of $5, $10, or $20 so you won't need dollar bills.

Another important thing to consider is how you are going to secure your tree inventory overnight and other times when you are not out there. If you are operating from home, you might be able to store the trees in the garage overnight. Perhaps you only exhibit representative sizes and keep your main inventory at the back of the house or in the garage organized by height (however, you will want to be sure to exhibit enough trees out in your sales area so passersby understand you have a good selection).

Lastly, you will need to spend a little money on some advertising of some kind, especially if you do this from home and home is a little out of the way. If you are renting a corner of the strip mall on a busy highway, you may have enough drive-by traffic to generate enough sales—and a few of those people will their friends and family members. But otherwise, an ad in the paper starting the week before you will be selling and going until just about Christmas Day is a good idea. You will also want a big sign, preferably with a giant green tree on it. People will get the point.

MARKETING ANGLE

In most Christmas tree sales operations, but especially those of the cut-your-own variety, you need to market more than just the purchase of a tree—you are selling a family experience, a future memory. Make sure your marketing literature and website have pictures of families (with their permission) having fun picking out their tree and driving away with a tree on the roof of the family van and a happy family inside.

NICE TOUCH

If you operate a cut-your-own tree farm, have a supply of those gel-pack hand and toe warmers. Buy them in bulk and sell them to your customers.

People will spend more time, and therefore more money, if they are comfortable!

Also, whatever kind of operation you have, plan to have a decorated tree. Consider selling tree stands that you think are the easiest and best to use. See if there are crafts-minded people who want to sell ornaments or, if you have a warm shed nearby, have a craftsperson conduct a class in ornament making once a season.

EXPANSION POSSIBILITIES

A Christmas tree operation has a natural expansion to selling other Christmas decorating-related products such as wreaths, kissing balls, tree toppers, and ornaments plus handmade items such as tree skirts and decorations for the house.

WORDS TO KNOW

Choose-and-cut: A type of Christmas tree sales where customers pick out their own live tree and either cut it themselves or have tree farm staff cut it for them.

Leader: The top vertical branch of an evergreen tree that grows each year and from which horizontal branches sprout. Leaders are an important part of the annual trimming process; trimming them as the tree grows helps the tree become more full and less tall and sparsely limbed.

Pre-cut: Selling Christmas trees that are already cut, usually utilizing a parking or vacant lot for the Thanksgiving-to-Christmas selling period.

RESOURCES

National Christmas Tree Association, www.christmastree.org

DAYCARE

28

Perhaps you love children. Perhaps you have children of your own and the idea of taking care of a few more for part of the day appeals to you. If so, then a daycare business might be just the business for you.

Childcare needs continue to soar in the United States. Many people prefer the option of their child being cared for in a home environment while they are at worked, opposed to a more institutional-like setting. These things mean that a homebased childcare business can get off and running immediately.

HOW THIS BUSINESS IMPACTS YOUR HOME

The impact on a childcare facility in your home is quite substantial. If you have a room that is separate from the rest of your house or an addition that has a separate door, that would be optimal.

THINGS TO CONSIDER

Be sure to consider how parents will drop off and pick up their children. If your morning household is busy, having children being dropped off at the kitchen door can add a lot of confusion. If you have a room with a separate door that parents can use, this can solve both the problem of not disrupting the rest of the household as well as your not having to leave the other children under your care while you greet an incoming child.

Be sure your neighborhood's zoning allows for a childcare operation. You also want to check your homeowner's insurance policy; you will need a rider for this kind of business.

HOW DO YOU WANT TO SPEND YOUR DAY?

You need to want to spend most of your day with several children. Unless you take on enough kids to justify hiring help, you will need to run your own errands and make appointments for yourself in the off hours. Work towards to hiring help, because you will need backup if you or your own child has an emergency that needs to be tended to or need to take a sick day.

WHAT YOU WILL NEED

First, you will need an impeccable reputation. The space where the kids will be needs to be clean, clean, clean—hire a cleaning service if this just adds too much to your schedule. Plan to have a bookcase full of children's books, as well as a wealth of safe toys and a toy box to store them in. Naptime is critical—have extra blankets, sleeping bags, and pillows available in case parents don't bring their child's own.

Install a few shelves in the room that can store kids' lunch boxes out of reach (you don't want a peanut-allergic child to get into another kid's lunch).

MARKETING ANGLE

Your biggest marketing angle with a home-operated daycare is that the parent can feel comfortable knowing their young child is spending the day in a home environment. Show pictures of happy kids playing, eating snacks, taking naps, and feeling at ease in your home daycare.

NICE TOUCH

You can have people come in to conduct classes with the kids in art, crafts, dance, etc. at various times throughout the week. During this time, you can be cleaning, making a few phone calls. catching up on e-mail—whatever you need to do. Encourage kids to bring home a piece of artwork or something they made. Or use a digital camera to take a picture of each child during dance class and print it out from your computer for them to take home. Maybe even during the next craft class they can make a frame for the picture to give to mom or dad on Mother's or Father's Day!

EXPANSION POSSIBILITIES

You probably will want to start of slowly in the daycare business, taking on just a couple kids at first. Your expansion will come as you can handle more children and perhaps eventually hire someone to help; the child-to-adult ratio should stay small so kids are always being supervised. You will need to expand to the outside as well, with a fenced, safe playground for children to play in when the weather is nice.

WORDS TO KNOW

Anaphylactic shock: This is a potentially life-threatening form of allergic reaction that requires immediate care. Children can be allergic to common foods and pets, so be sure to learn of any child's allergies and keep note of them in the child's records.

Background check: If you hire any help for a childcare business, it is important that you do a thorough background check on the employee before letting them work in your daycare business.

CPR: Cardipulmonary resuscitation. Check with any Red Cross or your local EMTs and firefighters to see if there is a local class you can take to learn CPR. And be sure you learn the specifics of performing CPR on small children.

E.C.E.: Early childhood education. It is a marketing benefit to your childcare business if you have some E.C.E. experience.

RESOURCES

daycare.com

childcare.net

29 APPLIANCE REPAIR

$$

Every household has a number of appliances, large and small. Dishwasher, clothes washer and dryer, refrigerator, stove, and freezer comprise just the basics. Other small appliances like fancy coffee makers, garbage disposals, window air conditioners, toaster ovens, and microwaves mean that the work available for a well-rounded appliance repairperson is almost endless.

You can work on your own or on contract with appliance stores to cover their warranty service calls—or best of all, you can do some of each. You will need to plan to start slow and build your customer base on recommendations and referrals based on work well done. Consider developing relationships with contractors to be the go-to person to install appliances in newly constructed houses.

Make up business cards and post them in restaurants and grocery store bulletin boards where homeowners frequent. Unless you plan to specialize, become familiar with all kinds and all brands of appliances so you will not be stumped when someone calls with an unusual appliance make or model.

HOW THIS BUSINESS IMPACTS YOUR HOME

Because most of your work will be done in other people's homes, the impact on your home is not substantial. You should have some storage space for parts, tools, and accessories, because you can get better prices if you buy commonly used items in bulk quantities. You want to have a space where you can work on one or two appliances in your home, but this isn't necessary—it is rare that you are going to have to remove an appliance from a customer's house.

THINGS TO CONSIDER

Appliance repair undoubtedly requires the ability to do some heavy lifting. Appliances are commonly tucked into tight spots—you usually will not be able to work on a washer, dryer, or refrigerator without moving it first. Don't count on many of your repairs being at shoulder height; you will need to bend over, kneel down, and lay on the floor quite a bit.

HOW DO YOU WANT TO SPEND YOUR DAY?

Appliance repair can be like figuring out a puzzle. Sometimes it's an easy puzzle, sometimes it is not. While you will spend most of your time interacting with the inanimate appliances, you can't forget that your customers are human beings. In order to stay in business, you need to understand customer service as well as, if not better than, most businesses.

WHAT YOU WILL NEED

You need the expertise to repair appliances, of course. You can take courses at community colleges, do-it-yourself home stores, and even online. If you do warranty work, the appliance company may offer courses for free or a modest fee. You can also learn a lot by just taking apart old appliances—check with any used appliance business; they commonly get drop-offs of all kinds of appliances that either work or not. Many new appliances have computerized systems, so it is important to keep up to date on all modernizations of appliances.

You will need a basic computer work station to keep track of appointments and billing and client information. An internet connection will allow you to look up appliance repair manuals, many of which are now online. You will also need a phone service of some kind to get your jobs; a cell phone is probably best since you need to be available while out on the road.

You will definitely need a vehicle that can accommodate some tools and a supply of common parts. It also should be able to carry a dolly, or hand truck, even if you have to hang it off the back of the vehicle on something like a bicycle rack.

Have a magnetic sign made that you can affix to the side of the vehicle so anyone who might be looking for an appliance repairperson knows you exist.

Be sure to take good care of your body. Purchase a back brace to protect your back while lifting, knee pads to help when you are kneeling on ceramic tile and concrete floors, and a warm vest and a pad for the floor for working in cold basements. You may want to develop a relationship with a chiropractor or massage therapist; you will want to be able to be seen on a moment's notice if your back needs attention. This can help you avoid injury and get back on the job faster when injuries do happen.

MARKETING ANGLE

Repairing rather than replacing appliances is a good way for people to save money, and a good marketing angle for you. It's also good to go green and promote that fixing something rather than throwing it away is good for the environment

NICE TOUCH

Bring along the appropriate cleaning equipment for all kinds of appliances. When you are done repairing the appliance, leave it cleaner than when you arrived. This nice touch will not go unnoticed!

EXPANSION POSSIBILITIES

There is only so much one person can do, so unless you plan to hire staff, expansion in this business is probably reserved to adding as many customers as you have time for and perhaps taking on contracts such as warranty work for a major appliance provider.

WORDS TO KNOW

Troubleshooting: Locating the cause of a problem.

Warranty: The guarantee of the integrity of a product, for which the maker will fix or replace parts or the entire product within a pre-determined period of time.

RESOURCES

Uncle Harry's Appliance Repair Shop (www.appliance-repair.org) offers a program for learning appliance repair and starting your own business.

RepairClinic.com is an online source of parts, tools, and instruction directed toward the do-it-yourselfer (www.appliancerepair.com).

30 CHIMNEY SWEEP

Any chimney that is used for a fireplace or woodstove needs to be cleaned annually. That means a lot of business for a chimney sweep. This business is pretty easy to start but difficult to carry out, since you will spend most of your time on roofs.

Learning to be a chimney sweep may mean nothing more than apprenticing with someone already in the business. Of course, you won't want to learn the trade from a chimney sweep in your intended market area, unless it is someone who is planning to get out of the business and would appreciate some free help in exchange for telling you everything he or she knows.

The sweeping itself is not too complicated. The tools available make it fairly easy to do. But you need to know about different chimneys and how they are set up, as well as techniques for shielding the fireplace opening to keep soot and dust from entering the house. You should plan to clean the fireplace hearth in the inside of the house as well as the chimney itself.

You need to learn about chimney construction, brick work, and mortar. By becoming a chimney expert, you can combine a chimney sweep business with a chimney inspection service—covering more than just whether or not the chimney needs cleaning but whether the chimney is in good working order or in need of repair. This service could be of use to home inspection services—an inspector may have general knowledge of chimneys but if a chimney seems to need repairs beyond the general inspector's expertise, he or she may recommend to the homeowner to have the chimney checked out more carefully by someone with more knowledge. Chimney sweeps also want to have some expertise in woodstove use.

One way to have steady business is to work on contract for landlords who have lots of rental properties. If you live near the ocean, a lake, or a ski resort where there are lots of seasonal homes, market yourself to these homeowners to clean their chimneys once a year to ensure that they can safely sit by the fire or heat up their second home with their woodstove.

While you don't want to instill fear, marketing your services from the safety angle is a good way to convince people that having regular chimney cleaning service is a smart and safe thing to do.

HOW THIS BUSINESS IMPACTS YOUR HOME

Keep your chimney sweeping business completely out of your house. You need a vehicle that can carry ladders and your equipment around, and can store your equipment while you are not using it. Wear coveralls and remove them before going in your house. If you have room, it is worthwhile to install an inexpensive washing machine to be used only for the clothing you wear for your work.

THINGS TO CONSIDER

You will be dirty most of the time while you are on the job. Have seat covers in your vehicle that can be cleaned at often, and perhaps are inexpensive enough to toss out and replace once a month. Or consider using paper seat covers that you dispose of daily.

HOW DO YOU WANT TO SPEND YOUR DAY?

If you enjoy being outside most of the time, chimney sweeping is a business that can be fulfilling. It is also physically demanding work, as you will be climbing ladders and working in high places a lot of the time. You will also need to spend some time each day fielding calls to line up work.

WHAT YOU WILL NEED

You will need chimney cleaning brushes of varying sizes to accommodate a variety of chimneys. You will also need a substantial ladder to ensure that you can get up to any roof you come across. Don't rely on homeowners to have ladders; having your own equipment is the best way to go.

You will also need bonding insurance to ensure to the property owner that if you fall off their roof, they would not be liable.

MARKETING ANGLE

The cost of fuel is not going down, so heating with wood is going to be more popular than ever. Market the safety angle of having a chimney in good repair and clear of creosote buildup. Promote the benefits of wood heat for saving money and diminishing reliance on fossil fuels.

NICE TOUCH

When people think of chimney cleaning, they think of dirt. Many people worry that their homes will be covered in soot after their chimney is cleaned. If you make sure that the homeowner can't even tell you've been there, you will have a lifelong customer ready and willing to pay for the safety service of having their chimney cleaned.

EXPANSION POSSIBILITIES

While you're up there on the roof cleaning the chimney, there are other services you can offer, such as installation of chimney caps and minor chimney repair such as brick repointing.

WORDS TO KNOW

Chimney swifts: Small mosquito-eating birds that build their nests on the inside walls of chimneys. They typically migrate to North American starting in March and fly south by early November.

Creosote: The byproduct of wood burning, this sticky substance can build up in a chimney to the extent that it can light on fire from embers from the fire and cause a dangerous fire known as a "chimney fire."

Liner: Some chimneys are lined with metal, tile, or concrete to prevent fire embers from getting between cracks in the brickwork of the chimney, and causing a fire.

RESOURCES

The Chimney Safety Institute of America (www.csia.org) certifies chimney sweeps. They offer training and marketing programs to help chimney sweeps as well as provide education to homeowners.

31 COMPUTER REPAIR

Hardly a building exists in America that doesn't have a computer in it, and many have more than one. When computers break down, they need to be repaired. Most computer users are lost if their computers are on the blink, and few computer users know how to repair their machines themselves. Many people use computers for their income, and thus a down computer means lost work time.

How do you learn about computer repair? Many community colleges often offer computer repair courses. And, with the proliferation of obselete equipment that can be hard to dispose of, you could easily get old computers to pull apart and learn how they work on your own.

Another aspect of computer repair is being a consultant in computer purchasing. If you have no connection to a particular brand of computer, you can be the unbiased opinion when it comes to what system a buyer should purchase. Learn about all the computer brands: Dell, HP, Compaq, Acer, and Apple, to name a few.

Study the main types of software that system users will want—word processing, photo manipulation software, mail merge, spreadsheet, design, and especially security software. Investigate all the components—monitor types in all their varieties; keyboards, from wired to ergonomic to wireless; mouse types; as well as peripheral components like printers and scanners.

Become completely familiar with all the ISPs (Internet Service Providers) available in the market area you plan to cover. This will enable you to get your clients up and running once you have helped them decide on the right system and components for them.

People love what computers can do for them, but few people want to learn more than how to operate them. Establish yourself as the guru who can meet the needs of the personal computer user, the small business, or a larger corporation.

HOW THIS BUSINESS IMPACTS YOUR HOME

You need a clean and well-lighted space to work on computers. It doesn't have to be huge, but you need a work area that allows you to spread out any parts you remove. Preferably this space will have a door that can be closed to keep the cat, dog, kids, and dust and dirt from the rest of the household out of the room. Although computers aren't nearly as delicate as they were just ten or fifteen years ago, it is still important to work in as dust-free an environment as possible.

THINGS TO CONSIDER

For consulting work, you want to interview potential consulting clients to figure out what system is going to work best for them. Create interview forms for each type of client you will have, from personal to small business to corporate clients with several users and a networked system.

You can do phone interviews and input the information straight to the digital form. You can choose to mail, email, or fax the form to clients and have them fill in the basics. Or you can meet them in person to get the information you need. Whichever way you choose, you still want to walk them through some of the information because they will not know the terminology to use and you can ask additional questions to help draw the right information out of them.

HOW DO YOU WANT TO SPEND YOUR DAY?

If you combine repair with consulting, the computer business can be a nice mix of working with people, doing detailed work on computer repair, as well as doing internet and in-store research. If you just do computer repair, be prepared to spend your time doing a lot of close work and having little interaction with people.

WHAT YOU WILL NEED

You can either do this business on the road or set up shop in your home. Either way, you will need a space in your house where you can work on computers. If you have a spare room, set up a sturdy table with good lighting.

You may decide to attempt to fix the computer at the person's home or place of business and if it proves more complex than can be fixed on the road, you can take the computer back to your home repair shop. In the case of corporate customers, they may have an open, well-lit space where you can work. If you do lots of repairs on the road, you will need a portable case full of all the tools you may need. You can equip a tool briefcase and use those tools both on the road and for home repairs, so you don't have to (at least at first) acquire two sets of tools.

MARKETING ANGLE

If you can become the quick go-to person for someone whose computer is suddenly on the fritz, you can become quite the hero! Market yourself as always being there for your customers.

NICE TOUCH

A nice touch in the repair business is to spend a few minutes cleaning each computer you repair before you return it. Use compressed air to clean the keyboard, clean the fingerprints and smudges from the monitor, and clean dust and dirt out of the computer itself.

EXPANSION POSSIBILITIES

In the repair business, one of the simplest expansion ideas is to sell components. You can also give classes in computer use, perhaps helping users avoid some of the pitfalls they encounter.

WORDS TO KNOW

Firewall: A software or hardware protection system that prevents certain traffic from flowing into your computer.

Memory: The ability of your computer to remember what you save on it. Memory can be installed in different increments; the more memory a computer has, the faster it will operate and the more data it can store.

Mother Board: The primary circuit board that makes your computer work.

RESOURCES

Parts source for computer manufacturers, sparepartswarehouse. com

Resource for computer repair technicians, technibble.com

32 ELECTRONICS REPAIR

This business is similar to the computer repair business, but you will take on all sorts of electronic equipment besides just computers. These days that means a huge amount of items, from iPods and MP3 players to cell phones, televisions, printers, scanners, and stereo equipment. Today even small electronic equipment is expensive enough for people to consider paying for repair over replacement.

With smaller electronics, you will need to be prepared to have customers bring their repair projects to you, as you would have difficulty recovering the cost of driving around picking up broken equipment and returning it.

You will want to create flyers and business cards that you can post in the usual places around your market area—grocery store and restaurant billboards are two places where the general population may see your advertising. One of your big jobs will be convincing people to have their small electronics repaired rather than just replacing them. You may also want to encourage people to give you their old electronics so you can use them for parts. Don't put a drop box in front of your house and open that up to just anyone—you soon will not be able to drive into your driveway with the amount of small electronic devices overflowing into your yard!

HOW THIS BUSINESS IMPACTS YOUR HOME

You will need a dedicated place to work on these projects that is clean, clutter-free, and well-lit. You will need shelving to store repair jobs in the works and you will need a system to keep track of whose equipment is whose.

As mentioned above, you will want a space that is amenable to people dropping off and picking up their electronics. It's best if you don't have to stand at the kitchen table and explain what you did and accept payment while your spouse and kids try to eat their dinner.

THINGS TO CONSIDER

You need to make sure your homeowner's insurance covers this type of business traffic. This is the kind of business where eventually you might consider taking on a small inexpensive retail space in a higher-traffic area. You could still do a lot of your repair work in your home, but the retail space would be open a few hours a day to accommodate drop-offs and pickups. You can pay a high school kid to staff the space for you for a few hours in the late afternoon or evening and Saturday mornings, which is probably the most likely time people will be dropping off and picking up.

HOW DO YOU WANT TO SPEND YOUR DAY?

This can be quite detailed work; some of these electronics can be pretty tiny! And you will most likely be performing all of your work indoors.

WHAT YOU WILL NEED

Set yourself up with a nice work area that is pleasant to be in and takes your health into consideration. Be sure your immediate work area has excellent task lighting; you will also want a head lamp, perhaps even a magnifying head lamp. You will need a set of tools similar to those needed for computer repair. And you will need to find a way to become familiar with the insides of the latest in electronics—either by taking a class, or finding cast-offs that you can pull apart and learn on your own—perhaps both. You will also need a computer system to handling your billing and keep track of your business.

MARKETING ANGLE

Although these electronics can sometimes be quite small and seem disposable, they are also quite expensive. Promote that they are something worth repairing and there are options to just throwing them out.

NICE TOUCH

Do some bartering with retail establishments to put up advertising at their site in exchange for a discount on any electronics repairs they may need.

EXPANSION POSSIBILITIES

Start small, working on one type of small electronic appliance and expand to more items. You can also eventually work on computers, which will expand your business quite a lot.

WORDS TO KNOW

Bluetooth: A short-range wireless communications technology enabling electronic devices to communicate with each other.

iPod: A digital audio storage and playback device created by Apple.

MP3: MPEG-1 Audio Layer 3; a digital audio encoding format used for audio storage.

RESOURCES

Parts source, allelectronics.com

Questions and answers, repairfaq.ece.Drexel.edu

HAIR STYLIST

Hair styling is a popular business that can be quite lucrative. Generally a homebased hair stylist business is likely to be started by someone who has already has a cosmetology career and wants a change. If you already have your cosmetology training and license, and loads of experience under your belt working in a hair styling salon, you probably have a following who will follow you right home without any hesitation.

HOW THIS BUSINESS IMPACTS YOUR HOME

Having a homebased hair styling salon will have a significant impact on your home. While you will probably be the only stylist, you will want to have two hair cutting and drying stations so that you can have customers overlap. It all depends on how much room you have.

You can renovate a spare room, an addition, or a heated porch into a salon. The salon can be pretty simple in décor but you will need, of course, electricity and running water. It is best to have a separate entrance so customers do not have to come into your home to have their hair done.

You can consider keeping this a very low-key business and doing hair for, say, just older folks or children. These clients are less likely to be bothered by your salon being set up in your kitchen. But this isn't where the hair styling money is either!

THINGS TO CONSIDER

You need to be sure you did not sign a contract with the salon with which you were working that prevents you from soliciting your clients to continue with you when you leave. However, a percentage of your clients will leave the salon on their own because people get very attached to their stylist, so the salon is going to lose these customers anyway.

HOW DO YOU WANT TO SPEND YOUR DAY?

If you follow the best path for making this a homebased business, you already know all about what it's like to be a hair stylist and how your day will look—but now it will be in your own home! So when that client calls last minute to cancel the appointment because she is sick or because of an emergency, or perhaps a client just plain forgets, you are right in your own home where you can make the best use of that unexpected down time.

WHAT YOU WILL NEED

Plan to have a separate room with two simple styling stations, mirrors, one hair washing sink, lights, and a chair for color setting. The room can otherwise be simply decorated with an easy-to-clean linoleum floor. Plan to have a small amount of shelving in case you want to sell products; a good way to add a little income. Styling equipment can very easily be bought used or leased.

You'll need a phone and computer for making appointments and keeping track of sales and the small amount of product inventory you will keep on hand. And a simple music source would be nice as well.

MARKETING ANGLE

If you were a stylist at a salon, make sure your customers know they will get the same great service at your new home location. You will need to promote the fact that you have as nice a setup as you did at the salon.

NICE TOUCH

If you have young active people as your customers and give them coupons to hand out to their friends, you will build your business with more customers like them. Also consider doing a loyal customer promotion, where every 11th (or whatever) haircut is free. This is especially good for male customers, who cut their hair more frequently.

EXPANSION POSSIBILITIES

You won't be in a position to expand your home salon too much—and besides, there is only one you to do all that styling—but you can branch out into more lucrative work such as focusing on hair styling for the bride-to-be. This may mean going to them instead of them coming to you, but hey, you may want to get out of the house once in a while anyway.

WORD TO KNOW

Depilatory: A chemical product that removes unwanted hair.

Emollients: The ingredients in shampoos and other cosmetic products that smooth and soften.

Root lift: Creating "volume" by using products or styling appliances such as curling irons and blow dryers.

RESOURCES

salonfurniture.com

buyritebeauty.com

34   SMALL ENGINE REPAIR

Repairing small engines, from lawn mowers to snow blowers and everything in between, can be a lucrative and busy homebased business. Most of the small engines you will work on will be easily transportable machines.

If you aren't already one of those mechanically minded people, you will want to get some training. Most community colleges offer some level of engine repair courses. Another way to learn would be to take a part-time position at a repair shop or a rental facility where you could learn on the job, although you will want to be open about your plans. Some businesses may not want you to work for them and then start your own business; some may be busy enough that not only are they happy to help you learn small engine repair, but they will send business your way when they are over capacity themselves.

You should be prepared to work on push-behind lawnmowers, riding lawnmowers, generators, garden tools like rototillers and edgers, chainsaws, wood chippers, and snowblowers. You need to decide whether you'll want to take on bigger jobs like tractors, snowmobiles, and/or ATVs; space may be your decision-maker.

Small engine repair can be a very busy business. Be prepared for a seasonal onslaught of business and learn to be cheerful about it. When a huge snowstorm is predicted for the day after tomorrow, you will suddenly have a flood of customers wanting their snowblower fixed. Sure, this could have been addressed a month before the big storm appeared on the radar screens, but you don't need to add to their stress level by reminding them of that. Cheerfully take their call, put them at ease, and be realistic and honest about whether or not you envision being able to fix their machine by the time the storm hits. You create a lot of goodwill if you either give them a list of other small engine repair places they might try or if you have a few machines around to rent out to your customers (inexpensively for those who are having work done with you) like the auto body shops do for those with cars in for several days for repairs.

HOW THIS BUSINESS IMPACTS YOUR HOME

The biggest impact on your home is that you will likely have customers bringing their small engines to you. This means having the appropriate insurance for customers coming to your home and the right space to accommodate them.

You could solve this by offering pick-up and delivery service, but that would mean you would spend a significant amount of time running around. This may be fine in the beginning, but as your business grows, you may want to spend your time working on engines, not toting them around. If you have a driving teenager in the house or the neighborhood that would like to make extra money by doing the pickup and deliveries after school or on Saturdays, this could be a way around having much traffic at your home. You could pass the cost along to the customer and offer this as an extra service. But you would probably need to provide the teen with a truck and/or small trailer to do this service—this may involve some auto insurance issues that you need to investigate before going this route.

THINGS TO CONSIDER

Be sure your driveway has plenty of room for customers to come and go with their repair work. Most likely, this will involve pickup trucks and perhaps ramps. If your driveway isn't a cul-de-sac type where someone could drive in and turn around, your street should to be quiet enough for a truck to stop on the street and back into your driveway for ease of unloading.

Doing engine repair means the smell of fuel and greasy hands. Many mechanics have taken to wearing rubber gloves to keep their hands as clean as possible. The fuel smells may mean you may not want to choose the garage bay closest to the door to your house if you have a connected garage—the smells will get into the house.

If you live in a northern climate and do this work through the winter (remember, those generators and snowblowers need repairs and the garden equipment will often be coming to you during the off season), you will want a heated space in which to work.

HOW DO YOU WANT TO SPEND YOUR DAY?

Small engine repair can be quite physically demanding. You need to get the tool that the engine is contained in off the truck or trailer and up into your work space, and to avoid constantly bending over or kneeling, you will want to have a waist-level work surface.

WHAT YOU WILL NEED

You will need a space devoted to small engine repair. The best and easiest scenario is to carve out a space in your garage. You will need both open space for repair work and some storage of machines awaiting repair while you wait for parts to arrive or can fit them into your schedule. You will want a small amount of storage for common parts and products such as cleaners, spray lubricants, etc. Make sure you have organized tool storage. Tools will be important—start with the basics since tool purchases can quickly run you over our $5,000 limit, and you will always want to buy the highest quality tools you can manage to afford.

MARKETING ANGLE

Like electronics and appliance repair, the marketing angle with small engine repair is the benefit, both to the wallet and the environment, to fix something rather than throw it away. Market your services by telling potential customers how their machine will operate better than ever!

NICE TOUCH

Always give the customer their equipment back cleaner than when it showed up. If you don't have time or interest in cleaning, hire that same teenager who does some delivery and pickup for you to come in a couple afternoons a week and clean any piece of equipment ready to go back out the door. This is the kind of thing that will give you that all-important word-of-mouth advertising when customers tell their friends and family about your above-and-beyond service.

EXPANSION POSSIBILITIES

Starting small and focused with a homebased business is always a good idea. If you start out your small engine repair business doing just, say, lawnmower engines, you can then begin to expand your services to all other small gasoline engines, then perhaps add diesel engines to your repertoire. That way your customers can plan to bring all their small engine repair needs to you. You could also move into larger engine repair such as tractors, but you may need to purchase an expensive trailer to move them around with, and you will nee room in your yard or garage to work on a piece of equipment the size of a tractor.

WORDS TO KNOW

2-cycle: A 2-cycle engine has one power stroke for every turn of the engine, opposed to a 4-cycle engine where all four pistons must stroke in turn to complete one power cycle.

Cylinder block: The part of the engine that contains the piston, crankshaft, and all internal components.

Valves: Flaps in the engine that allow the air-fuel mixture to enter the cylinder; the valves are positively sealed when closed.

RESOURCES

Education, smallenginerepair.com

Troubleshooting, small-engines.com

HOUSEHOLD ORGANIZER 35

Who doesn't need this service? You may have to do some marketing that convinces people of the benefit of paying for you to come in and organize their homes (many people always think they are going to find the time next weekend...), but once you snag their business, the value of your services will spread like wildfire.

You can choose to either do the organizing work or to come in to a home and consult on the things the homeowner could do to better organize. You may be consulting on garages overstuffed with sports equipment and junk; countertops whose actual surfaces haven't been seen for months; clothes closets; kitchen cabinets; home offices; laundry areas; garden sheds—the list of potential spaces that could use organizing is endless.

Have a portfolio of different organizational scenarios in different rooms in the home and talk with the homeowner about the style they like. Would they like to see all their clutter organized in a series of baskets that fit neatly under a bench in the kitchen? Or does that seem like clutter to them too? Would they rather see everything packed out of sight in cardboard boxes?

Create checklists and questionnaires to understand how the family uses the home. Are the kids wildly busy with after-school activities? Or are they usually home after school and want access to their toys? What kinds of activities are members of the family into? Do they share rooms? All of these things will help you tailor an organizing plan and become the family hero. There is no use helping someone organize if the organizational plan is not something they can stick to.

HOW THIS BUSINESS IMPACTS YOUR HOME

You will do most of this kind of work outside your house. You will want an office space in your home where you do research and keep a supply of catalogs that contain organizing tools that you can recommend to your clients. You may choose to stock and sell some of these organizing products—if so, you will need space somewhere in your home to store a small inventory.

THINGS TO CONSIDER

While this business is homebased and you work for yourself, you will be out on the road much of the time doing your actual work. The marketing, billing, and research will be done from your home office.

HOW DO YOU WANT TO SPEND YOUR DAY?

Much of your day will be spent in other people's homes. You need to enjoy interacting with people and have impeccable interpersonal skills as well as the ability to help people become at ease with something they may be a bit embarrassed about.

WHAT YOU WILL NEED

You will need a reliable vehicle on which you might want to put a magnetized business sign. You will need to come across as incredibly organized yourself—you won't get much business if you open your car door on arrival and piles of papers, old coffee to-go cups, fast food wrappers, and books come tumbling out!

MARKETING ANGLE

Make sure all of your marketing materials are incredibly organized and neat! No typos, no grammatical errors—nothing says disorganized more than a ratty looking brochure full of errors. You need to project the image of what you will be helping your clients become.

Then take your marketing literature and go where the busy people go—grocery stores and restaurants. These are two places where people who are busy might be attracted to your solicitation. They are in the grocery store thinking how many other things they could be doing with their time, such as clearing out the clutter of the house, and they go to restaurants because they are either too busy or their kitchen is too messy to cook!

NICE TOUCH

Provide your customers with a newsletter and/or other literature that helps them stay organized once you have put their lives back in order. Offer an online Q&A session or other ongoing help that will make them feel less abandoned after you leave.

EXPANSION IDEAS

A good way to expand in the organizing business is to sell the organizing products that you recommend to your clients.

WORDS TO KNOW

Binder: A notebook used to bind together similar paper items such as recipes, photos, or letters to make them more easily accessible.

Filofax or DayRunner: A brand of appointment calendar that contains various organizing compartments include the calendar and notepaper as well as a modified wallet system.

Organizational systems: Usually refers to systems of racking and other items that help clear and store items that otherwise create clutter.

RESOURCES

organize.com

Organize magazine, organizemag.com

LANDSCAPER

Everyone wants a lovely yard and few people have the time it takes to make that happen. This is where your love of gardening and outdoor work and your ability to envision landscape possibilities will pay off in a great business. You can get a degree in landscape design, but if you have a knack for this type of work, a degree won't be necessary. Most people want their yards tidied up in the spring, their lawns mowed in the summer, their leaves removed in the fall, and their shrubs and driveways ready for winter snow.

These are the basics that a landscaper should offer, but you will also want to offer garden work such as

- flower bed cleaning and preparation
- spring planting of annuals and perennials
- summer weeding
- vegetable garden preparation, planting, and fall cleanup
- fall bulb planting
- fall bulb removal of sensitive plants
- spring replanting
- pest control
- watering

Beyond flowers and vegetables, you can offer tree care service such as

- dead branch removal
- pruning of fruit trees and berry bushes

- planting of new trees
- tree health care such as pest control and disease care
- keeping limbs away from roofs of all buildings

And there is plenty to do in the yard that has nothing to do with plants:

- stone wall restoration
- fencing—perimeter, garden, and decorative fencing
- walkway creation and repair
- gazebo and garden shed construction
- irrigation system installation

The ideas of services to offer with this business are as endless as the different yards you will encounter. Of course, the more money you want to make, the more you will need to market your services to affluent communities.

HOW THIS BUSINESS IMPACTS YOUR HOME

There are two main ways the landscaping business impacts your home. First, will need space to store a trailer or truck full of your landscaping tools. Second, your own home landscape will need to be neat and well tended, if not stunning. The first thing you might want to do before starting your landscaping business is completely renovate your own home landscape. Put pictures of it on your website and invite potential clients to drive by and view your yard. If you don't have a yard or it is not visible to customers, plan to renovate a couple yards at cost. Pick ones that are in high traffic areas that potential customers can see on their way home from work.

THINGS TO CONSIDER

Landscaping and yard work is physical labor at its best—not overly strenuous but enough to know you have done a day's work. Keep yourself in good shape. Always use safety equipment like chaps and a helmet with ear protectors and a face shield while operating a chainsaw. Get a high quality set of knee pads for all the kneeling work required when planting and weeding flower beds. Wear sunglasses to protect your eyes and sunscreen and clothing to protect your skin from harmful UV rays. Protect yourself from ticks and Lyme disease by wearing light-colored long pants tucked into your socks and inspect yourself at the end of every work day.

Also, landscapers often work in tight neighborhoods. If you need to tow a trailer to haul riding lawnmowers and other equipment, try to always pull the trailer off the road into a driveway. If you have to, unload it and park in a nearby parking lot or neighbor's driveway (with permission). Landscaping trailers on narrow roads can be a danger and gives a negative impression of your business.

HOW DO YOU WANT TO SPEND YOUR DAY?

By nature, a landscaping business will have you working outside every day all day, rain or shine—and snow if you choose to offer snow removal. You will need to enjoy being outdoors and not mind getting dirty.

WHAT YOU WILL NEED

Don't feel like you have to buy everything—rental stores abound where you can rent tools like a post hole auger for a couple days. Renting tools gives you a chance to try the tools out, allowing you to gain a better understanding of what features are important to you when you go to buy your own. However, if the tool is something you will use often, it is something you want to buy soon before your rental costs exceed what it would take to buy the tool. Consider buying used, even from the rental store itself.

You will need a home office for a computer workstation in order to do scheduling and billing, as well as a business phone line.

MARKETING ANGLE

A nice yard where homeowners can relax after a long day's work is a real draw for this business. Remind potential clients in your marketing literature that you can do the yard work while they are at their jobs and over the weekend they can sit in the gazebo and admire their lovely property. Some people like to do yard work but they just don't have the time for all of it, so let them know that you can leave the things that they like to do and take care of the rest.

NICE TOUCH

If you are hired to do year-round work for customers, create a customized calendar for them showing roughly when you will do certain work. You don't need to pin it down to a day or even a week; a list of what services you will do within a certain month is sufficient. Have the calendar feature a picture of their own yard at its most beautiful. These kinds of calendars are easy to create using a simple computer system.

EXPANSION POSSIBILITIES

You can start this business concentrating in one area of the yard—like lawn care or flower gardens or spring/fall cleanup—and then expand your reach into other aspects of landscaping as you get established.

WORDS TO KNOW

Aerobic: Needing oxygen to survive. This term is usually used in reference to composting—aerobic organisms in compost break down the material into good soil.

Bedding plants: Bedding plants are typically flowers that are planted massed together to create an attractive flower bed.

DIY: Short for do-it-yourselfer, where homeowners do their own yard work and home repairs. A landscaper should probably expect clients who want a mix of the things done for them that they don't like to do or don't have the equipment to do along with things left for them to do themselves.

RESOURCES

landscaping software, adkad.com

lawnsite.com

37 MASSAGE THERAPIST

Massage therapy is fast becoming an appreciated therapy to maintain good health. Clients range from those who do physical labor to those who sit at a computer all day to elderly patients and everyone in between; they all recognize the physical and mental health benefits of massage. Now is an excellent time to get into this fast-growing field.

You will want to become certified in massage therapy to be able to effectively market your services. Courses that lead to certification include not only information on human anatomy and physiology and the effects that massage has on both, but also on how to make a business out of the field of massage. You could do either a certification program or an Associate's degree and stay within the $5,000 scope of this book.

Be sure to have business cards printed and a sign created for your massage business (check local zoning for signage regulations). Offer free massages to family and friends and watch the word spread.

If you are not a naturally tidy person, you will need some help in this area. People are not going to feel comfortable unless the massage area is almost clinically clean. If you can't accomplish this, plan to hire a cleaner to do daily cleaning of your business area. Perhaps you have a teenager in the house who would love to earn some extra money spending an hour each evening cleaning your massage room, doing laundry, restocking oils, dusting the art work, and cleaning the glass in the mirrors and windows. The room should always look impeccable and smell wonderful.

HOW THIS BUSINESS IMPACTS YOUR HOME

A homebased massage business will have a significant impact on your home. You will definitely need a separate room that is used for nothing else except your massage business. This room needs to be kept immaculately clean—no dust, dirt, or cobwebs. It should be able to be isolated from the rest of the household.

For the utmost in professionalism, this room would have a separate entrance, is quickly accessed from a hallway or foyer, and has easy access to a bathroom.

THINGS TO CONSIDER

A massage business means you will be dealing with laundry. You will need enough clean laundry to change the sheets on the massage table after every client. Clients will need blankets for covering themselves and towels to wipe excess massage oils off before putting their clothing back on.

While getting a massage may be relaxing, giving a massage is a strenuous job. You need to be in good physical shape and be able to use your hands for a good portion of your work.

HOW DO YOU WANT TO SPEND YOUR DAY?

Massage therapy is by nature an intimate human contact job. You need to be comfortable with people and bodies of all types. You will need to have supreme interpersonal skills and know how to make people feel comfortable. If all of this appeals to you, and the idea of helping people live healthy lives gives meaning to your work, you might enjoy massage therapy.

WHAT YOU WILL NEED

Your massage business, as stated earlier, will need a dedicated room in your home. The room needs to big enough to accommodate a standard massage table of around six feet long by two to three feet wide, with space around all the sides for you to move around as you work. Tables range in price from around $400 to over $1000, the higher end including pneumatic legs operated by a foot pedal.

The room will also need a chair or clothes rack or hooks on the wall for clients to hang their clothes while getting their massage. You will want a dresser or table of some kind to hold oils and perhaps a candle. Except for the massage table, the room can be easily furnished for little expense.

Massage oils are pretty much the only products you will need, unless you plan to offer facials and other add-on services.

You might want to have an air purifier in the room. These are often quiet and help add to a clean, peaceful environment. Depending on your house, you may need a window air conditioner in summer (these days, decent window units can be had for just a couple hundred dollars; if your window can't accommodate an a/c unit, there are floor models that cost a little more) and a small (quiet) space heater in winter.

Plan to have a small piece of stereo equipment of some kind and a supply of calming CDs—if you have an iPod, you can load it with some appropriate music and purchase decent speakers for under $100. Paint your room a soothing color, hang some curtains, and put a couple rubber-backed throw rugs on the floor.

Finally, you need to have a business insurance liability policy that covers massage therapy. Some states have insurance requirements that you will need to be aware of before opening your doors.

MARKETING ANGLE

The rushed world in which we live today makes a massage appealing to people who want to slow down a little. Also, massage therapy has known health benefits. Add testimony from reliable health sources to your marketing literature. Testimonials from happy, healthy clients is always a good thing too!

NICE TOUCH

Many service businesses lend themselves to frequency clubs—offer a half-price or even free massage every ten massages. And offering discounts for massage referrals can bring in business more quickly.

EXPANSION IDEAS

You can expand your massage business by offering different kinds of massage or adding other health-spa type items to your menu, such as facials. Or if you have the space, add a sauna or hot tub for your clientele to use.

WORDS TO KNOW

Body mechanics: How the body parts function together. Massage therapy can help improve body mechanics.

Edema: Collection of excess fluid in cells. Massage therapy can help alleviate edema.

Palpation: Conducting an assessment through touch.

Range of motion: How far the joints can move is referred to as range of motion. Massage therapy can help improve range of motion.

RESOURCES

www.massageproducts.com offers oils, scrubs, linens, massage tables and many other massage-related products

38 UPHOLSTERING

$

Furniture is comprised of four basic components: the framework, a spring system, the padding that covers the spring work to make it comfortable, and the covering, usually called upholstery. Some upholstery is leather, but typically it is a durable fabric.

If you have a knack for sewing, upholstery repair might be a perfect business for you. You need to have some understanding of furniture construction. One of the best ways to learn how to upholster is to get some discarded upholstered furniture and start tearing it apart. There are techniques to make sure your work is high quality and there are tools to help make your work easier. Many books and some videos are available to help you learn this trade.

Often furniture ready for upholstering will also need repairs. You can request that the owner have these repairs made before they deliver the piece to you for upholstery work; have a list available of furniture repair people you can recommend to your customers. Or you can take the piece in, have repair people you work with do this work for you, and you add it to the overall cost. You can also learn to do this work, especially minor repairs, yourself. Most furniture repair work does not require expensive, large, or complicated tools. But it does require some skill.

You will also need to figure out how to work with the customer regarding fabric for your upholstery work. You can recommend upholstery fabric sources to them and let them pick out their own fabric, buy it, and bring it to you. If you decide to work this way, you will need to figure out for the customer how much fabric to purchase. Or you can choose to work with a wholesaler, get swatches to show to clients, and order the fabric for them.

Furniture upholstering is fun and creative work. Although there may be some minor lifting and physical needs involved with moving the furniture around, you can typically hire local high school kids to move the largest pieces for you. The rest can typically be maneuvered with a hand truck and some, like dining room chairs, are small enough so that they can easily be moved around.

HOW THIS BUSINESS IMPACTS YOUR HOME

You can get by with carving out a spot in an extra room to work on your upholstering projects. However, you may need some space to store clients' furniture as it comes in for upholstering. You can get around that by scheduling your projects so that no more than a couple pieces are on site at any one time. However, there may be times, when you are waiting for fabrics to arrive or glue to set, that you will have more than one or two pieces in your possession.

THINGS TO CONSIDER

Although this work shouldn't require much in the way of insurance, you do need to ensure that valuable antiques are covered.

HOW DO YOU WANT TO SPEND YOUR DAY?

Upholstering is close work, and you will be inside most of the time.

WHAT YOU WILL NEED

Equipment needs for upholstery are not extensive. You will want more than one pair of very high quality scissors—i.e., ones that cost $50 instead of the $6.95 ones you buy for the kitchen. Button cutters and machines allow you to create upholstery buttons out of the fabric that is being used. Other upholstery tools include a ripping tool, pliers, curved and straight needles, hammers, foam cutters, staple pullers, and upholstery pins. Chairs and sofas have webbing under the seat; these are installed with a webbing stretcher. You can purchase most of these tools for a total of well under $1000, probably closer to $500. Your biggest expense will be an industrial-grade sewing machine; used ones can cost upwards of $2,000. Buy the best you can afford and upgrade as you gain customers.

MARKETING ANGLE

This is another business where you can appeal to people's desire to do good by the planet and recycle things rather than toss them out and buy new. Plus, the cost of reupholstering a sturdily built piece of older furniture is almost always less that buying an as-well-built piece of new furniture. Promote the "preserving family heirlooms" angle as well.

NICE TOUCH

Always send furniture back not just with new upholstery but the wood elements polished and the whole piece looking new. You want your customers to say "wow" when they see their beautifully renewed piece of furniture. After all, the piece had to be special enough to recover instead of replace.

EXPANSION POSSIBILITIES

You could add minor or even major furniture repair to your repertoire. You could also get into cleaning upholstered furniture that doesn't necessarily need to be reupholstered.

WORDS TO KNOW

Cambric: The light gauze-like cloth used underneath the seat portion of a chair or sofa that covers the springs.

Tacking: The pounding of small nails, called tacks, to attach the upholstery fabric to the wood frame of the furniture. These days, stapling is done more than tacking but the term is used for both.

Webbing: Flat strong fabric pieces that provide support under support seats and springs.

RESOURCES

New and used industrial sewing machines, shop.raphaelsewing.com

USED BOOK SALES

Almost everyone has a few boxes of books stashed away in the house somewhere. Why not make a business out of them? If you don't have enough books to open up shop, check with friends and family members for their stashes, too. Instead of paying them for the inventory, offer them a gift certificate to your shop when you open the doors.

In order to gain customers—especially repeat customers—you will need to have some regular shop hours. Set yourself up a computer workstation in your shop or purchase a laptop with a wireless card and set up wireless internet capabilities. During your downtime, you can go online and research used or remainder book inventories for sale or post some of your choice selections on eBay. Set your shop up with a website on which you list your inventory and rotate showcasing some of your finer selections.

Make your shop known for something—a specific category (or two) of books, having some first editions for sale, all paperbacks a dollar and all hardcovers two bucks, and/or a swap program. Booklovers love used bookstores and they also have lots of booklover friends who they will tell about your shop. People looking for books are always interested in other printed materials as well—maps, illustrations, postcards, greeting cards, and magazines are good sidelines to include in your shop. Perhaps you or someone you know makes bookmarks—these are great impulse purchase for a buck or two at the counter.

HOW THIS BUSINESS IMPACTS YOUR HOME

This is the kind of business where having an outbuilding such as a garage or barn or shed that can accommodate the business is important. You don't want people coming into your home and rummaging through your personal collection of books.

THINGS TO CONSIDER

You can get quickly overrun with used books. Be discriminating—and remember, even the library refuses free books after a while, as they just don't have the room.

This business doesn't take a lot of capital to start but it also doesn't offer huge income unless you get into something like the first edition business.

HOW DO YOU WANT TO SPEND YOUR DAY?

This is not a business that you will need to have open every day. Get your customers accustomed to your hours and they will come when you are open. This is a type of retail business and you will spend your time indoors during shop hours—unless you can catch a few rays reading in a chair by the shop door when you have no customers.

WHAT YOU WILL NEED

Other than a room of some sort to sell the books, the things you will need for this business are bookshelves, bookshelves, and more bookshelves. You also need a cash register and a credit card account with your bank to be able to accept credit cards. You may want a couple chairs for customers to be able to relax while they are in your shop. If your space is a converted outbuilding, you can probably get away with heating it with a space heater.

MARKETING ANGLE

Promote the recycling-at-its-best angle of this business! To market your business, consider starting a monthly book discussion group. Have people come in, buy a book (at discount if they are a member of the group, perhaps), and sign up to provide a commentary on the book at the next meeting.

NICE TOUCH

Offer a search service to help customers find books. In this computer age, almost everyone is internet-savvy, but some people might want you to do their searching for them, especially if you hitch up with an affluent collector.

Another thing you can do to help drum up business is start a book club or reading group—maybe an unusual one where everyone reads a different book and talks about what they liked or didn't like about it.

Have some free coffee, tea, and snacks and encourage visitors to browse for a while.

EXPANSION POSSIBILITIES

Many people's homes are overflowing with books and there are rarely enough bookcases to hold them all. Offer an exchange program—take home one book for every two you bring in to be sold. Or consider a consignment program. This business is expandable to the amount of space you have. If you get serious about old books, you can get into the book repair service, rebinding leather books and repairing broken bindings. You can begin a locator search service for people looking for a specific book. You can also set up shop on eBay and sell books there, as well as on Amazon.com.

WORDS TO KNOW

Boards: The cardboard pieces used as the foundation to create a book's hard cover.

Gutter: The interior edges of the page of a book.

Preservation: The restoration of an old book to as near original condition as possible.

RESOURCES

bestconsignmentshopsoftware.com

eBay.com

Amazon.com

40 BUSINESS PLAN SERVICE

Every business, small or large, needs a business plan, and an expert at pulling business plans together will always be in demand. There are literally dozens of great books about business plans from which you can learn the basic elements and go from there.

This is a business where you will need to network in all the right places. Tell everyone you know about your service. Join the Chamber of Commerce in your city and surrounding areas; attend their events and hand out business cards. Become familiar with your local SBA. And definitely market your services online—this is not a business that needs to be restricted to your local area. A few phone calls, e-mails, and perhaps one in-person visit (and many times even that is not necessary) and you can pull together everything you need to create a great business plan.

You may want to specialize in a certain kind of business, but don't put yourself in too narrow of a category. Being general is better, such as being an expert in the retail industry, service industry, or manufacturing. Offer a soup-to-nuts business plan, including market research, the business plan narrative, and the financial statements. You can target business plans to different recipients—a bank for financing, individuals for a potential active partner, a corporation for silent partner. Each will require slightly tailored versions of the business plan. Plan your fee around the main one that the client will want and offer the others as add-on services. You can then -tweak the main business plan accordingly. You can give the client an electronic file (either via e-mail or on a CD) and allow them to take it from there, or you can keep the business plan on file and offer the service of tweaking the it for the client whenever necessary.

Have business plan samples to show clients—and make sure to include your own! Collect business plans in many different industries (make sure to black out the business name), collect them in magazine holders or a file cabinet so that they continue to look neat and fresh, and replace them as soon they get worn or outdated. Another place to find sample business plans is in books about starting your own business.

HOW THIS BUSINESS IMPACTS YOUR HOME

This business should have very little impact on your home besides the space for a workstation and the ability to talk on the phone with a degree of privacy.

THINGS TO CONSIDER

You will spend a lot of time sitting in front of a computer creating business plans. You will also need to be comfortable with crunching numbers when creating the financial statements necessary for a comprehensive business plan.

HOW DO YOU WANT TO SPEND YOUR DAY?

Again, this is one of those businesses where you will find yourself in a chair staring at a computer screen a lot of the time. The beauty, as mentioned previously, is that you can get up and stretch your legs—run errands, bring your daughter to soccer practice, or take a run on the beach with the dog—any time you feel the need. You can also get some face time with real humans by attending functions and events where potential clients may be lurking.

WHAT YOU WILL NEED

You need a decent computer with comfortable components (ergonomic keyboard and large-screen monitor, for instance), a comfortable workstation with a well-designed chair, and a desktop with some room to spread out.

You will also need a business phone with a hands-free headset or speaker phone to allow for long conversations you will have with clients.

None of this takes a lot of space, but you may want to have a room where your office can be separate from the family living space so that you can talk on the phone undisturbed and so you can spread out and not have to pick everything up each time you leave the room or the house.

MARKETING ANGLE

Remind potential clients that they are experts in their industry, but you can be their "business" expert. Having a fresh eye look at their business will provide them with a comprehensive business plan.

NICE TOUCH

Follow up with clients to see if their business ever took off, and if so, how things are going. You might include an extended service that allows them to come back to you to update their business plan a couple years down the road, perhaps in order to expand into a new area or to get more financing.

EXPANSION POSSIBILITIES

One way to expand is to write separate marketing plans for your business plan clients.

WORDS TO KNOW

Niche: A small portion of a market to whom you can target sales.

Return on Investment: Also called ROI, this refers to the profit you get on something based on how much you paid for it or it cost to produce it versus how much you sold it for.

Turnover: The number of times an inventory of goods is sold during a given period.

RESOURCES

business-plan.com

bplans.com

One way to make money in this field is by being an expert witness yourself. If you have an expertise that could be useful in legal cases, you can market yourself to attorneys to act as an expert witness.

Another way to be active in the expert witness field is to play a sort of matchmaker, matching attorneys up with expert witnesses for their cases—either for the defense or for the prosecution. Almost any kind of expertise can be needed in the legal arena. More common are psychiatrists and psychologists as well as almost any medical doctor. Dog behavior experts can be used in dog bite/attack lawsuits; automobile repair experts can be called upon to testify in vehicle accident cases; plastics experts may be helpful for lawsuits regarding children's toy mishaps. The list is almost literally endless.

These are the people you see represented on the television court cases where one side or the other calls a witness to simply testify as to the accuracy of certain testimony according to the expert's knowledge of the field in question, and lend his or her expertise in adding background knowledge and understanding for the jury's sake.

You will want to keep a database of all experts you begin to compile. When lawyers come calling, you can contact the appropriate potential expert witnesses and find out who is the best person for the job and who can fit it into their schedule.

Expert witnesses for big money cases can be expected to fly anywhere to testify. There's no reason your database of witnesses can't be from all parts of the country, so even if you are based in Florida and a lawyer from Seattle contacts you, you might have an expert on your list who lives in Portland, Oregon, and can easily testify in the case.

Plan to have a website and offer your experts some tips on testifying, how to dress, how to answer questions, and information on what will be expected of them from the lawyers for whom they will be testifying.

You can make your money in a couple different ways. One is to charge the attorney a fee and you pay your witness. Or the attorney can quote their fee, pay the witness, and you take a percentage of that payment.

HOW THIS BUSINESS IMPACTS YOUR HOME

An expert witness service should have minimal impact on your home beyond basic office space.

THINGS TO CONSIDER

You need to market your services. Also, needs for expert witnesses can come up at a moment's notice so you need to check your voice mail and e-mail several times a day.

HOW DO YOU WANT TO SPEND YOUR DAY?

You will spend most of your time on the phone and the computer. This means being locked in your office for much of your work time. However, the usual work-at-home benefits of being able to get up out of the chair and run errands or whatever applies.

Make your business line a cell phone and you will always have contact with your business. If something urgent comes up, you can take your laptop with wireless internet connection and stop at any one of the hundreds of locations in any given area that now offer free wireless service.

WHAT YOU WILL NEED

You will need an office space that affords a certain amount of privacy. Legal cases are usually confidential. Clients need to be assured that this confidentiality is being maintained. You will need a speedy computer with plenty of memory to accommodate a growing database of names and information. You should plan to construct a website so attorneys can easily find you.

MARKETING ANGLE

Your marketing is pretty straightforward with this service—attorneys are the ones who need expert witnesses. They are an organized bunch, so plan to rent a mailing list or e-mailing list. Plan also to have a website, and mention your website on all your marketing materials.

You can also target your business to a certain topic or industry, such as pet liability lawsuits or the oil industry. This will depend on what your background is and it does narrow your marketing and your market.

NICE TOUCH

Helping your witnesses understand the process with things like information sheets on your website and e-newsletters is a nice way to show support beyond just locating their next job. They will appreciate you remembering that they are the ones out there literally in the hot seat. Also, follow up with a phone call after the trial to see how things went and ensure that your witnesses are being treated appropriately.

EXPANSION POSSIBILITIES

If you begin with a narrow market or focusing on one industry or legal category, you can eventually expand by branching out into other categories. If you have access to expert witnesses in several categories, you will certainly create more business opportunities.

WORDS TO KNOW

Forensic medicine: A science that deals with applying medical facts to legal problems.

Jury: A body of people chosen through a legal process to hear both sides of a legal case and render a verdict.

Perjury: The act of lying under oath; perjury is a serious crime.

RESOURCES

Look at other expert witness referral businesses, such as:

Round Table Group, roundtablegroup.com

Medical Expert Witnesses, naclncdirectory.org

42 MARKETING COPY WRITER

Business owners know their own businesses inside and out. But when they try to put their business down on paper, you start to wonder if they really have any idea of what they do. Doing it and explaining it are two different things. And typically, when they try to explain their business, they want to include every tiny fact and figure, thinking that customers actually care about that level of detail. Customers care about how the business benefits them. Marketing and advertising copy writing experts understand this.

Marketing and advertising copy is not the same as other kinds of writing. There are ways to grab attention and ways to turn people off. If you can write copy that gets people excited about purchasing what your client has to sell, you can make good money in this business.

Unless you are highly experienced from working in the copywriting field, take a course. There are online courses or classes at community colleges and universities that can give you a leg up in getting savvy at writing copy for brochures, catalogs, advertising, and, of course, marketing copy for the web.

HOW THIS BUSINESS IMPACTS YOUR HOME

This is another homebased business that requires nothing more from your home than a small but comfortable office space with a decent up-to-date computer and high-speed internet capabilities. Client interaction can happen almost exclusively via phone and e-mail, with occasional in-person visits at the client's site.

THINGS TO CONSIDER

You will need to learn how to write snappy copy. If you consider your writing pedestrian at best, you'll want to get some help. You can take or refuse any jobs that come your way, but you may find yourself someday being asked to write about products that you don't believe in. If you have certain things you can't bring yourself to write about—perhaps you are a vegetarian for whom the idea of writing for the beef industry would be distasteful—consider focusing on industries that do interest you, and that you already know something about.

HOW DO YOU WANT TO SPEND YOUR DAY?

Being a copywriter may entail a small amount of travel, but otherwise, plan to be sitting in front of a computer screen most of the time. You may also spend some amount of time browsing catalogs and other marketing copy from your client's competitors, but even a good amount of that can be done online. (Although bringing a tote full of catalogs to the beach or the local coffee shop is certainly an option.)

WHAT YOU WILL NEED

You will need a basic up-to-date computer that has plenty of memory. Plan to get high-speed internet access into your home if you don't have it already. And you will need wireless access if you decide you'd like to work from a laptop and have the flexibility of being in whatever location in the house inspires you. Do plan to invest in a few marketing copywriting classes, unless you have just retired from years as a copywriter.

MARKETING ANGLE

This is another business where specializing in a topic or industry will help get you started. This makes marketing easier to do. Pick a group of people that are reachable, who have an organization, or who somehow group together in a way that allows you to market to them as a group.

NICE TOUCH

Go into your meetings with clients (in person or via phone/e-mail) with a good amount of knowledge of their company under your belt. It's a plus to be able to say you are familiar with the product being discussed and jump right into the conversation.

EXPANSION POSSIBILITIES

Once you have mastered a certain industry, begin to write copy for others. After you have established yourself, you have samples you can send out and references to help you gain credibility in a new field.

WORDS TO KNOW

Blog: Created from the words "web log," a blog is an online journal created by anyone and usually about a specific topic.

Clients: The businesses for whom you do copywriting. You will not want to overlap businesses in the same industry, as you would essentially be helping rivals compete with each other.

Target Market: The audience to whom your copy is directed.

RESOURCES

For tips on writing copy for online marketing pieces, see Copyblogger at copyblogger.com

SOLAR ENERGY CONSULTANT

43

The time has come for alternative sources of energy to go mainstream. Even though solar installations are still on the expensive side, the price of fossil fuels is beginning to meet solar in the middle. This is a good business to get into, as this will be a lucrative market in the foreseeable future.

As a solar consultant, you can basically conduct a home inspection and give clients a report on their solar options for their particular home and site. While it pays to be an engineer to be able to really get in-depth with your recommendations, if you fully familiarize yourself with all solar options, you can give people solid advice and options to consider. This can range from full-fledged general solar installations that generate electricity to simple solar walkway lighting.

You might want to start by working in a solar products company to become knowledgeable in the solar energy field. However, to be a consultant, it is often best not to be affiliated with any one company or product and be able to recommend products and options across the field of solar energy.

Finding clients may be as simple as posting your business card around different places in your area, from restaurants to grocery stores—anywhere that people paying high fuel bills might see it. You can also advertise on menus, in weekly papers, and other low-cost advertising venues.

While you will want to be clear that you can recommend a full range of solar options and products from many different companies, you still want to be known to any solar energy companies in your market area. You are only helping their business.

HOW THIS BUSINESS IMPACTS YOUR HOME

You will need a computer workstation and storage space for brochures from solar product companies. You may also want to have a few small solar products on hand either for sale or to show potential customers.

THINGS TO CONSIDER

Don't expect customers to go the full solar route in one sitting. Plan your reports so that they can add on in stages, maybe starting with heating the carriage house that is used as guest quarters, moving on to solar-powered water heating, to perhaps a solar-powered whole-house fan. Explain what gives them the best bang for their buck right off, and what add-ons can be beneficial in what order down the road.

HOW DO YOU WANT TO SPEND YOUR DAY?

As a solar energy consultant, you will be working somewhat like a home inspector. You will go to a client's home (or business) and conduct an inspection of the premises in regard to how suitable it is to solar energy and, if so, what applications may work and solve their needs. You should plan to climb ladders and inspect roofs. You may not think you would need to spend much time in basements—after all, the sun doesn't tend to reach there—but you will be looking at how the solar energy can be tapped into the home's electrical or water system, so basements will be on your list.

WHAT YOU WILL NEED

You will need a reliable vehicle that can carry a ladder and perhaps a few small solar applications so clients can see products firsthand. Collect a stack of product brochures from each of the solar companies with whom you do business, so you can show clients a photo of a particular solar product in place—such as a photovoltaic panel on the roof of an outbuilding.

MARKETING ANGLE

With the ongoing trend toward green technologies, marketing solar power will not be difficult. People want to know what they can do to reduce their nonrenewable energy use. The biggest obstacle to overcome in the field of solar is the continued expense of the technology. Your marketing needs to target people who want to be green at any expense and your literature needs to make it clear where the savings are to make solar installation financially worthwhile. Research statistics and put graphs and charts in your marketing materials that reference legitimate sources to highlight the upside to solar energy.

NICE TOUCH

Install some solar applications at your own home and invite local customers to come see them. For those not local, take pictures and describe your reasoning for the installation you chose and your experience with the application. Get these kinds of testimonials from satisfied clients as well.

EXPANSION POSSIBILITIES

Once you become a solar expert with your successful consulting business, you will begin to pinpoint products that you feel are the best on the market. One expansion possibility is to sell these products. To become a distributor, you would need to stick to one company's products. But if you simply supply solar products, you can purchase inventory at wholesale and sell several different brands. Another area of expansion can be if you not only consult and plan solar installations but also actually install them. The learning curve there is a little longer, but if you find solar energy is your field, then you won't mind learning what you need to know to cover all aspects of the business. Another long-term way to expand is to become knowledgeable in other renewable energy technologies, such as wind and water power.

WORDS TO KNOW

Grid: The system of energy distribution. Solar power users are often looking to get off the grid.

Photovoltaics: Generating electrical energy from radiant (solar) energy. Solar panels often are referred to as having photovoltaic cells.

Renewable energy: Sources of energy that are either limitless, like solar, or can be regenerated, such as trees.

RESOURCES

Solar Energy International, solarenergy.org

Clean Energy Exhibition, solar.org

GOLF COACH

Are you a better-than-decent golfer? Do you love to play the game? Do enjoy learning the intricacies of this ancient game, and think you might like to pass that knowledge along? What better way to spend your time than coaching people who would like to enjoy golf more themselves by learning to play better.

You can start with your friends and family. There is someone there who wants to learn or has a kid who wants to learn how to play golf. When you get your coaching skills down par, venture out looking for new clients.

Let the local public courses know about your coaching business. Cultivate relationships with the staff and encourage them to recommend you as a coach. Of course, you will need to be careful not to appear to be stealing customers away from the pro, if the course offers lessons.

Another place to look for customers is the corporate world. Golfing is a game that business people use develop relationships outside the office. Many people want to be able to play well enough to simply not make a fool of themselves while playing with their boss or an important or potential client. And you can help them.

You do need to be a better than average golfer to develop a reputation as a golf coach. You also need to be a good teacher, know how to be motivational, and be willing to work with many different types of people.

HOW THIS BUSINESS IMPACTS YOUR HOME

Being a golf coach doesn't need to have much more impact on your home than having space to store a set of clubs. You might want consider having a computer workstation to be able to work on marketing or write a blog to help develop your client relationships.

THINGS TO CONSIDER

This is a business that will build slowly. It is doubtful you will have a full complement of clients overnight. You may want to keep your day job for a while and do golf coaching on the side have a sufficient number of clients to support a full business.

HOW DO YOU WANT TO SPEND YOUR DAY?

Being outside on the golf course on a sunny afternoon is pleasant enough. But you may also need to be there when it is windy, chilly, and maybe even a little rainy. Your clients are probably fair-weather golfers themselves, so you may find plenty of appointment cancellations on those less-than-sunny days. You probably won't have to be on the course in bad weather, but you will lose out on income on those days—another reason to have other elements to your coaching business, like a blog, a website with tips, or a subscription-based e-newsletter.

WHAT YOU WILL NEED

To create a viable golf coaching business, you need to be a better-than-par golfer. It would be helpful to have some level of golfing credentials beyond just playing on the weekends. Perhaps you have won a few tournaments—they don't have to be PGA tournaments, just local or regional tournaments are sufficient for coaching leisure golfers. At the very least, have a decent, recorded handicap at your own club.

If you want to coach year-round, you obviously need to live in a warm climate. Not much golf gets played in the north in the winter months! With a three-season business, you can extend your season with some indoor golf-related activity such as a golfing blog, a newsletter, or a website. For this you will need a basic computer system.

MARKETING ANGLE

The biggest marketing angle you will need is to be able to legitimately promote yourself as a good golfer. Develop brochures and promote your services through places business people go, such as chamber of commerce meetings or trade shows. Start a website and always put it on every printed piece you create. Put some editorial content on your website that will get people excited about golf and what you can do to help them.

NICE TOUCH

Those who are considering golf don't want to go out and buy a bag full of clubs until they are sure they are going to stick with it a while. But there are plenty of people who have golf bags sitting in their garage who didn't stick with golf for whatever reason—lack of interest, health problems, physical injury. Buy a few sets of used clubs of varying types and lend them to your clients for their lessons. Even rent the full bag to them for part of a season until they are sure they are ready to buy their own. Then offer (for a fee, of course) to accompany them to help with their purchase—another great thing to do in the off season.

EXPANSION POSSIBILITIES

If you can find a reasonable venue, offering golfing classes can be a way to expand this business. You could do some consulting, helping new golfers pick out their first set of clubs and equip themselves for the course, as well as teach them the basics. You might learn the fitness side of golf and help your clients develop a workout program to complement their golf game.

WORDS TO KNOW

Handicap: This calculation of a golfer's average score is used to make all golfers equal on the links.

Par: The standard score for a hole.

Slice: An golf shot that unintentionally curves sharply; when the curve is done intentionally, the shot is called a "fade" or a "cut".

RESOURCES

golfcoach.com

golfcoach.org

COMPUTER TRAINING 45

You may think using a computer is a piece of cake, but there are still many people out there who find computers intimidating. Consider a business that helps people get over their adversity to all-things-computer. One group that this can be particularly appealing to is people in their 60s and 70s who did not grow up with computers as an everyday appliance.

If you are proficient in both Macintosh and PC, you should offer training in both types of computers. If you are going to concentrate on just one, the PC is the more common choice and the least expensive for a newcomer, and being less user friendly than the Mac, offers more opportunities for you! You can tailor your teaching to the customer and help them learn the software that is going to be most useful to them; word processing, photo enhancement software, or business spreadsheets are just a few examples.

You could probably make a living helping seniors learn how to use the internet and e-mail to keep in touch with their loved ones, who are now commonly spread around the country. Composing e-mail, sending attachments and photos, creating web pages and digital scrapbooks all would be of interest to this group, and an intimidating undertaking for someone who is not comfortable with computers.

Err on the side of caution in this business. People do not want to know all the details about what makes a computer work. If they have some success using a computer to do something meaningful for them, they will become eager to use your services to learn more and more. But if you overload them with information from the beginning by explaining bits, bytes, and megapixels, they will stick to their paper and pencil forever.

HOW THIS BUSINESS IMPACTS YOUR HOME

The least home-invasive and least expensive way to conduct this business is to go to people's homes and teach them. It is also best to teach them on their own computers, if they have one. If they do not, you could charge them a fee to help them make the purchase, and help them set up and connect their equipment.

THINGS TO CONSIDER

You can conduct a class and teach several students at once. You could limit your class to those who you have already set up in their homes—make the class one on how to expand your knowledge beyond the basics that they would have learned from you in their home setting. To take the class approach, you will need to have a classroom setting with access to computers. This might be possible in a local school, if they have a computer lab that they are willing to lease out.

You could also consider teaching small classes in an assisted living environment—teach small groups of two or three residents for short periods of time to learn one aspect of the computer at a session, rotating through a few sessions with different groups. Most assisted living facilities have a public computer or two for residents; this can help them make the best use of it.

You will need to figure out how to charge for your service. Classes will be charged per student and you can elect not to hold any class that doesn't meet the minimum number of students to make it worth your while.

Consider being "on call" a certain amount of time to walk clients through problems—incorporate that service into your overall fee and promote it as a real benefit. For most computer neophytes, learning how to use the computer is not a problem but dealing with complications when they arise can be difficult, as computer messages are often in language that just doesn't make sense to them.

HOW DO YOU WANT TO SPEND YOUR DAY?

Helping people get the most out of their existing computer system or to learn how to become comfortable with computers is very rewarding. You will spend a lot of time in front of the computer screen, but unlike working strictly on a computer doing your business, you will be interacting with people all of the time.

WHAT YOU WILL NEED

You need to know a lot about using computers—not necessarily the internal structure and language, but the common day-to-day usage that the average person will want them for. Learn a lot about the most common applications and tailor your instruction to the uses of your specific clients. But you don't need to know everything; if something comes up that you don't know, tell your client you will find out and get back to them. And make sure that you do get back to them!

MARKETING ANGLE

There are many potential users to whom you can direct your marketing efforts. If you decide to focus on members of the senior set who are insecure about their ability to learn to use a computer, be sure to keep your marketing materials absolutely basic. Just when you think it is simple enough, simplify it even more. To get these clients, you need to be respectful of their needs and make it absolutely clear that they are capable of using a computer.

NICE TOUCH

Call your clients between classes to see how things are going. This is especially nice if you focus your business on the senior computer users. This group of individuals often does not like to bother people and so they will wait to use their computer again until your next scheduled session. A call in between may allow you to walk them through their roadblock and get them up and running again—and give them a lot of confidence.

EXPANSION POSSIBILITIES

Once you get your clients comfortable with using a computer, surfing the internet, and e-mailing their friends and family, you can promote further services, such as helping them learn new programs and new ways to use their computer.

Consider creating online tutorials. Web-based classes can expand your audience from the face-to-face clients to an unlimited numbers of students to be found via the internet.

WORDS TO KNOW

Hardware: The physical equipment that makes up a computer system, such as the monitor, the CPU, the printer.

JPEG: A common digital photo format which consists of a compressed image file.

Software: The digital products used to run a computer.

RESOURCES

Nonprofit source of computer lessons for seniors, computerseniors.org

Glendora Seniors Computer Club, gscclub.org

GRAFFITI REMOVAL 46

Graffiti is everywhere—on billboards, in public restrooms, under overpasses. Like everything metropolitan, where there are more people, there is more graffiti and more locations for graffiti. But that doesn't mean suburban and even rural areas are immune to this unsightly problem. Graffiti writers think of their work as art or use it to make a statement. But business owners whose property are subject to this "art" think of it as nothing but criminal vandalism.

Many solutions exist that rid surfaces of graffiti. Create an arsenal of cleaning products that can clean almost every kind of product (paint, chalk, markers) from every kind of surface (cement, wood, pavement).

The best way to conduct a graffiti service is to offer a subscription-like arrangement. Once a month or whatever interval makes sense for your client, go around to their property and clean off the graffiti. Charge them a monthly or quarterly fee and make it simple for everyone—they don't have to think about graffiti and you just do your job.

HOW THIS BUSINESS IMPACTS YOUR HOME

The most significant impact on your home for a graffiti cleaning business is storage of cleaning products. In order to get the best price possible, you will want to buy in a certain quantity. Clear a space in the garage or shed to store excess products, beyond what you will need in your business vehicle.

With the proliferation of low-priced retail outlets, you can easily purchase much of your cleaning equipment as you are on the way to a job. No need to have excess inventory of that kind of thing around.

THINGS TO CONSIDER

Graffiti often is found in areas that might be risky to work in alone, so consider having a work companion. At the very least, keep a cell phone on you at all times. And consider a self-defense course. Chances are you will need none of this, but you can never be too safe.

HOW DO YOU WANT TO SPEND YOUR DAY?

Graffiti cleaning can be physically demanding work. Your work will be outside a lot of the time; however, public bathroom facilities are major targets for graffiti, so the interiors of beach facilities, gas stations, etc. can keep you plenty busy!

WHAT YOU WILL NEED

You will need a supply of several different cleaning products as well as tools to use to clean—scrub brushes, mops, cleaning equipment with extension handles and buckets. You will definitely need a ladder or two and a vehicle that can haul them around (either use an existing vehicle or lease a truck or van).

MARKETING ANGLE

Create a brochure and market your services to the owner of any structure on which you see graffiti. Also, be sure to create at least an informational website where someone searching for "graffiti cleaning services" can find your contact information. You could include a few cleaning tips and certainly some ideas about why your service is the best one to choose. Also promote your services to businesses via mailing lists from the regional chamber of commerce. Consider doing talks about why cleaning up graffiti is important to a company's image and do a brief demonstration of what is involved in a clean up. And this is another business where it can be lucrative to promote yourself as a green company, if you are using environmentally friendly products.

NICE TOUCH

Take pictures of any graffiti you encounter. With digital technology, you can easily take pictures of every customer's surfaces every month (or quarter, depending on the rotation you set up) and store them on your computer. When you send their bill each period, add printouts of any pictures of graffiti you cleaned so they know that you are doing your job.

EXPANSION POSSIBILITIES

Combine your regular customers with one-time customers so that you have an uninterrupted cash flow. Also, provide editorial content for websites on cleaning unsightly graffiti for areas outside the one you service. You can also plan to expand beyond the area of service you start out with, doing a different area each day of the week.

WORDS TO KNOW

Bubble gum: Those proclamations that have been around forever and used to be carved in trees, where "Tony loves Gail."

Etching: Where an object is used to scratch graffiti into a surface such as metal or glass. This type of graffiti cannot be cleaned; glass will need to be replaced.

Tagger: Someone who creates graffiti, generally under an assumed name and using a recognizable style.

RESOURCES

Ideas for promoting your business, spokanegraffiti.com
organicenviro.com

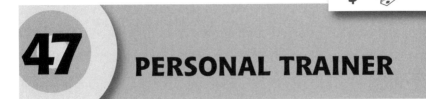

47 PERSONAL TRAINER

It seems everyone is either trying to lose weight or get in shape these days. The babyboomer generation is determined to stay as young as possible for as long as possible. That market alone could keep you busy as a personal trainer.

One way to get work as a PT is to align yourself with a fitness center. Many of them use their own staff as personal trainers, but some gyms in your area may make use of freelance PTs. Advertise your services in places where everyone goes, like restaurants and grocery stores. Having a website is a good idea—people want some privacy in their decision-making when it comes to getting fit. They can go to your website and determine if your approach to personal training is an approach that would work for them.

It is important to emphasize the safety aspect of using a personal trainer. You can help clients get fit and avoid injury. Using weight lifting equipment or even starting a fitness program without the advice of someone who is familiar with the equipment and exercises can be counterproductive. You also want to make sure any client you take on has gotten written approval from their doctor to start an exercise program.

HOW THIS BUSINESS IMPACTS YOUR HOME

It is unlikely you can set up a fitness center in your own home for less than $5,000. You want to go to clients' houses or meet them at the fitness center of their choice and work with them there.

THINGS TO CONSIDER

You need to be a fitness fanatic yourself. People who will hire you want to see that you practice what you preach and that your body exemplifies what you are trying to teach them. If you are showing them how to create the classic abdominal "six-pack," you should have one yourself!

And you need to be OK with working with people on a very intimate level. You need to be comfortable touching people and being in close proximity with them as you show them how to work out with machines and weights and the correct way to do exercises. It is one thing to enjoy working out yourself, it is quite another to show other people how to do it.

HOW DO YOU WANT TO SPEND YOUR DAY?

This will likely be a mostly indoor occupation. You need to enjoy the fitness center setting. You may be able to do a lot of your work in the evenings when people end their 9-to-5 work days, so you might be able to spend your daylight hours outside if that's what you prefer.

WHAT YOU WILL NEED

The most important thing you need is the ability to be upbeat and have great interpersonal skills. Criticizing people is not going to help them get in shape, nor is it going to help your bottom line—you need to have the skills to tell people what they need to hear in a way that they will actually hear it, instead of getting defensive.

You also need sound knowledge of nutrition and the human body. Take courses in sports training, anatomy and physiology, and nutrition. Community colleges with a nursing program will have these courses.

Purchase some portable exercise equipment and become skilled at using it. You don't need large exercise machines like treadmills and stationary bicycles—though some people have them in their homes. If your clients do, by all means make use of them, but you can do a lot with simple fitness equipment like jump ropes, medicine balls, resistance tubing, mini trampolines, and dumbbells. Many clients will want to have their own equipment, but be prepared with a couple sets to loan out until the client figures out which pieces they like.

On a safety note, secure dumbbells and other weight equipment in your vehicle when traveling around—if you got in an accident, you could have five-pound dumbbells becoming lethal weapons.

MARKETING ANGLE

Your approach will depend on what kind of fitness trainer you are and what kind of people you want to attract to your business. You can promote yourself as a hard-core drill sergeant to attract serious, highly motivated fitness buffs, or as a optimistic motivator to target people who would just like to lose ten pounds and be in better shape.

NICE TOUCH

Work with a registered dietitian to create a healthy diet program for your clients that promotes fitness and helps them have the energy level they need to do the routines you work out for them.

EXPANSION POSSIBILITIES

Like many consulting and service businesses, one way to expand in the personal trainer business is to sell fitness equipment. It would not take a huge investment to have a small inventory of medicine balls of differing sizes, several sets of dumbbells at different weights, jump ropes, etc. Take that one step further and buy larger fitness equipment like treadmills, stationary bicycles, even a Bowflex machine, and rent them out to clients to use for a couple months. This would also give people a chance to try these things without either having to pay the annual dues for a fitness club, or purchasing one of the machines only to find they just don't enjoy using it. With your rented trial, they can confidently buy what they like to use, and then you can rent your equipment to the next person. You can also provide consulting services to help them purchase the right equipment.

WORDS TO KNOW

Six-pack: Slang for well-developed abdominal muscles

Repetitions: The number of times you lift a weight in a set.

Set: The number of groups of repetitions in weight lifting. For example, you might do three sets of lifting a weight 15 times in succession.

RESOURCES

A wide array of sports equipment, sportsauthority.com

Personal trainer certification schools by state, naturalhealers.com

48 DESKTOP PUBLISHER

When calculators first became available to the general public, they cost over $100. Now you can buy a calculator that can perform pretty sophisticated math for $3.95 at the grocery store checkout line. Comparatively, computers are going the same route. Prices have easily halved in the last ten years and that new computer has several times the memory of its predecessor and lots more bells and whistles. This makes desktop publishing an attractive field.

While designing on the computer was once the sole purview of the Macintosh, the PC has become capable in design as well. And PCs continue to sell at a much lower price than the Macintosh. Only you can decide which computer system you are comfortable using—Mac users are often loath to be seen around a PC, and vice versa.

With either system, you can use desktop publishing software to create newsletters, magazines, books, or even marketing materials. And you can promote your services to others who have no interest in sitting in front of a computer and designing materials that will ultimately be in print (or published digitally, either as an e-book, e-newsletter, or online for web content).

If you are a writer, you can create the content for your desktop publications, or you can pay a writer to create the content for you. Alternatively, you can advertise your desktop publishing services to design and create newsletters and books for others with their content. You present them with the designed piece and they take care of the rest—printing and distributing it to their customers.

HOW THIS BUSINESS IMPACTS YOUR HOME

To make a viable business from desktop publishing work, you want an office space that allows you to have a good workstation. Plan a space that encourages creativity. It is best if you have an extra room in your house that you can turn into an office so you can work undisturbed.

THINGS TO CONSIDER

You need to enjoy the marketing side of things in order to create enough work for yourself in this field. That said, if you become good at it, you can figure on having plenty of work to create a thriving business.

HOW DO YOU WANT TO SPEND YOUR DAY?

Although you will be able to exercise the creative side of your brain, you will spend considerable time in front of a computer. Depending on what kind of publishing you get into, you also want to spend time looking at the latest trends and designs. If you focus on books, get out into bookstores regularly and study the types of books you are designing— every category of book goes through fads and trends. This kind of hands-on research will get you away from your desk/computer and out into the real world.

WHAT YOU WILL NEED

With the right computer, peripherals, and software, you will come close to the $5,000 startup limit with this business. For the basics, you will need the desktop computer, a large-screen high-quality monitor, and a better-than-average printer. The sophistication of printers has moved at a slightly slower pace than the computers that run them. That said, you can buy a very decent printer for well under $500. If you plan to print out your electronically designed materials, you will want a printer that has a high page-per-minute rate but still offers the highest print quality you can afford. Other peripherals include a scanner (approximately $200), a fax machine (approx. $150), and a photocopier, unless you have a copy shop nearby. All-in-ones (fax, printer, copier, scanner) are popular today, but for a business, you are better getting them each as separate machines.

You need a large work table or desk where you can spread things out, which can be had for a couple hundred dollars at any of the large office supply stores.

But the largest purchase you will probably make is for page layout software such as Adobe InDesign or QuarkXpress, each of which cost several hundred dollars. Add to that a basic business software package such as Microsoft Word, a subscription to a stock photo or clip art service, and a few useful or unusual fonts, and your software purchases could quickly run to a couple thousand dollars.

MARKETING ANGLE

The first thing you need to do is decide what kind of desktop publishing you want to do. If you want to design reports and marketing materials, promote yourself to the business community. Attend chamber of commerce meetings and hand out business cards. If you have a particular area of expertise or interest, then advertise in their trade publications or direct to members. For example, say you want to target attorneys. Advertise your services in your state's bar association newsletter. Don't forget to tell why it is beneficial for you to do their marketing literature for them—looking professional, knowing marketing language, and understanding design are just three benefits you bring to the table.

NICE TOUCH

Submit your projects to design awards—anyone you do business for will be thrilled to have their newsletter win an award. It's great publicity for both you and your client.

EXPANSION POSSIBILITIES

It's best to focus your efforts at first, but once you have some finished projects to show, you will be able to broaden your market much more easily. For instance, if you direct your beginning marketing efforts to attorneys via your state's bar association, you can then branch out to other states and the national bar (American Bar Association).

WORDS TO KNOW

AA or Author Alteration: Changes to a publication requested by the author. Authors are charged by the publisher or printer if they wish to make changes at the point where the book is no longer in manuscript form and is being prepared for printing.

Camera ready: A term that refers to material ready to be printed. These days, camera ready material is often in digital form.

Ragged: Where the lines of type are left uneven, referred to as RR or RL, ragged right or ragged left. "Justified" is when both sides of the line are flush with the margin.

RESOURCES

softwaremedia.com

Freelancer clearinghouse: Elance.com

49 MOVING SERVICE

How is your back feeling? If you are up to it, a service helping people move from one home to the other, from one office to the other, or even from primary home to second home and back is a business worth investigating. According to the website "Our Town, Inc.," 20 percent of the American population moves every year, totaling 43 million people. Americans move an average of 11 times in their lifetimes. And the typical mover has 56 items on their moving "to-do" list. That's where you come in!

Lots of people who are moving want to hire someone to do the heavy lifting for them. You can leave the large-scale, long-distance moving to the big moving companies. Your work can be the local, moving-across-town or to the town-next-door jobs. These are the ones that people start off thinking perhaps they could do themselves, and it will be your job to convince them otherwise. Your signs around town will tempt them to let you take care of that part of the move, while they are busy taking care of those other 500 items on their list.

Your most important attribute will be your reputation for treating your customers' possessions as if they were your own. This extra care means that the customer will find their things at their new home in the same condition they left them in at their previous home.

HOW THIS BUSINESS IMPACTS YOUR HOME

A moving service shouldn't have much impact on your home. You want to carve out some small space to have a computer to do billing and order supplies like cartons and packing materials. You may need space in the yard for a moving truck—even if you rent one only when you have jobs, you will probably want to get it the night before and park it at your house to be ready to go bright and early on the morning of the move.

THINGS TO CONSIDER

You should have liability insurance and be bonded for this business. Find out if your customers expect you to move anything that is extremely valuable, like original pieces of art, one-of-a-kind antiques and heirlooms, or pianos. At the very least, they should have insurance on those items themselves; you may even want to suggest they find someone who specializes in those kinds of items move the item before you come in to move the rest of the house's contents.

HOW DO YOU WANT TO SPEND YOUR DAY?

You'll be on your feet most of the time with this business, except when you are sitting in the driver's seat, driving the goods to the new home. You need to be willing to do heavy lifting and you need to enjoy trying to figure out the puzzle of moving large furniture around tight corners without damaging the furniture or the building.

WHAT YOU WILL NEED

You don't need to own a large truck in order to start this business. You can rent as needed from any of the major self-moving rental companies like U-Haul. This allows you to rent just the right size vehicle, instead of owning just one.

Instead of renting moving blankets from the truck rental company, buy a supply that you can use over and over. Be sure to unwrap items and remove your blanket from the site, or if you must leave them behind, plan to charge for them on the customer's bill. Buy a high-quality dolly or hand truck, or even two, along with some adjustable straps. These are especially helpful when moving appliances, and good ones cost in the $200 range.

You may want to purchase some packing materials such as cartons and bubble wrap. You don't need to get too carried away—if you live in an area where there is a supplier, you can wait to purchase these supplies when you look over the job and give the owner an estimate. Don't buy huge boxes thinking you can fit lots in them—they may be good for clothing and light items, but for dishes and books you want to have smaller sturdy boxes. Not only is it safer to transport small amounts of these heavy items, but it is better on your back.

Speaking of your back, be sure to purchase an industrial lumbar belt to support your back. These typically come with adjustable shoulder harnesses to help take the strain of lifting off your back. They are inexpensive at around $50.

You will want to have a few part time helpers lined up to assist you in this business. There are many aspects of moving you can do yourself, but when it comes to things like appliances, sofas, dining room tables, and woodstoves, it is not only almost impossible but unnecessarily risky to both your body and the customer's piece of furniture for you to try to move these kinds of things yourself.

MARKETING ANGLE

There is no question that you need to market yourself as taking care of your customers' possessions as if they are your own. When they open boxes in their new home, their things will be neatly and expertly packed. The main reason a homeowner will hire you to do the move for them is that the idea of doing it themselves is exhausting. Create marketing materials that show people in their new homes relaxing with a glass of wine by the fireplace after your company has done the hard work for them.

NICE TOUCH

Have an extra lumbar support belt in each size—small, medium, large, and extra large—in order to offer your helpers back protection. If you work in the same areas a lot of the time, prepare a packet of information such as directions to the grocery store, a list of dry cleaners, local breakfast spots, etc. This is the kind of thing that people who have relocated need to find in their new area.

EXPANSION POSSIBILITIES

You could expand your services to include specializing in moving antiques and expensive items. Or you could branch out to moving not only homeowners but businesses as well.

WORDS TO KNOW

Damage: The simple fact of an item arriving at its destination in a different condition from when it was picked up at its original location.

Lumper: A person hired by the mover to help load or unload goods.

Replacement cost: The cost to actually replace an item with a new one, not the original cost of the item.

RESOURCES

backsupportsystems.com

movingsupplies.net

50 INTERIOR DECORATOR

If you love to decorate and know about decorating styles and color schemes, an interior decorating business can be just right. You can offer your services to both homeowners and businesses.

Market your talents to building contractors. People purchasing new homes can often be overwhelmed with the choices and possibilities in home decorating. You can help them weed through the massive selection and end up with a décor they just love. It may cost them a little to hire you, but you will save them time—and we all know time is money! Not only will you save them time poring over catalogs and shopping in decorating stores, but you can also help them avoid having to return things they decide they don't like. In the inevitable cases where that does happen, you can do the returning for them.

The areas where people have the most trouble making decisions is in lighting, wall coverings, and flooring. These are big expensive decisions. One of the most complex rooms in the house is the kitchen—you can have a whole business based solely on interior decorating in the kitchen. Picking out countertops, cupboard designs and styles, sink types, and appliances is a massive undertaking.

Design some questionnaires for each major element and each major room in the house. Find out how the homeowner will use the home—are there children? Pets? Does the woman of the house wear high heels? Do the home's residents neglect to remove shoes? How will each room be used? Where might task lighting and ambient lighting be most appropriate?

Most homeowners like to have some fun with decorating their homes, so you can promote your ability to take care of the larger-scale needs, while leaving the smaller decorating choices—pillows, baskets, artwork, etc.—to the homeowner, with your help if needed.

This is a fun and exciting business with so much involved that it is likely you will never be bored!

HOW THIS BUSINESS IMPACTS YOUR HOME

You will want to be able to spread out lots of product brochures and catalogs. A computer workstation will be necessary so you can do online searches. It might be helpful to have a home situation where it is suitable for clients to visit you at your office. Alternatively, you can lease a van to keep your information with you to make it easier to work in the client's home.

THINGS TO CONSIDER

You need to have a cheerful personality and like to help people who may be feeling a little stressed out. They are probably hiring you either because they are moving into a new home or they are redecorating their existing home for a big event.

HOW DO YOU WANT TO SPEND YOUR DAY?

This business will be a mix of a lot of running around shopping for products and visiting clients as well as sitting in front of your computer searching for the best products to present to your clients. It may be the best of both worlds.

WHAT YOU WILL NEED

You need the standard computer setup. Get a good quality printer with a high page-per-minute rate for printing out product information from the internet. And you will need high-speed internet access. As mentioned earlier, leasing a van may be helpful not only for carrying around lots of product information, wallpaper books, upholstery swatches, and flooring samples, but also to have room to have a small supply of products such as lighting options.

MARKETING ANGLE

You could choose to specialize in one kind of decorating style, such as country, contemporary, or Arts and Crafts. You could also focus on one room of the house; kitchens are a good choice as they are complicated. Bedrooms are another good choice, since most homes have several, and bathrooms can be as well, especially if the redecorating includes some renovating.

NICE TOUCH

Have names of reliable contractors whose work you can recommend to do the painting, wallpapering, wiring and lighting installation, and flooring to your specifications. Once you have designed the decorating scheme for a home, stop by after the work is done and swoon over the client's newly decorated home.

EXPANSION POSSIBILITIES

If you start out focusing on one style or one room of the home, expand your repertoire to other styles or other rooms. Another way to expand is to get into retail decorating—this requires a whole new learning curve that involves knowing what makes people actually choose to buy.

WORDS TO KNOW

Primary colors: Red, blue, and yellow; colors that are mixed to create other colors but themselves cannot be made from other colors.

Sectional furniture: Particularly relating to sofas, this is created in separate pieces and designed to be mixed and matched, used separately or in conjunction with each other.

Slipcover: A piece of fabric that is designed to cover existing upholstery either to protect it or to conceal the original color/design to create a new look.

RESOURCES

interiordecorating.com has a selection of all things relating to interior decorating

decoratingden.com, the popular decorating franchise

51 MUSIC LESSONS

$$

Musical talent has always lent itself to providing lessons. If you are skilled with a musical instrument, consider offering lessons. You can choose to offer lessons to kids or adults or both, if you are comfortable switching from one teaching style to another.

You want to stick to the instrument(s) you know, but you may be a skilled enough musician to offer lessons on several different instruments, or those in a particular class, e.g., stringed or woodwind.

You can decide to take on individuals or classes, depending on space and availability of instruments. Public schools are continually reducing their commitment to art and music classes for students, so you can try to work with the public school system to supplement their efforts in those areas.

HOW THIS BUSINESS IMPACTS YOUR HOME

You will most likely want to give lessons at your home. You will need an appropriate space to do that, depending on the type of instrument you teach. Clarinet lessons, for example, don't involve the same space requirements as piano lessons.

You will also need to consider other family members. Are they willing to listen to an aspiring saxophone player squeeze out lots of bad notes with the good ones? Perhaps you can give lessons during times when no one else is usually at home, but there will occasionally be someone home sick from work or school which may cause you to have to cancel your lesson for the day.

THINGS TO CONSIDER

You will need to decide if you want to work with young potential talent whose motivation level may be coming from a well-intentioned parent or with adult students who have decided to take lessons of their own volition.

HOW DO YOU WANT TO SPEND YOUR DAY?

There is little opportunity for being outside in a music lessons business. That may be fine with you. But if you worry about being too cooped up, remember that music lessons don't have to take up your entire day. If you are working with school-aged students, your lesson schedule won't begin until mid afternoon. Working adults may appreciate some evening hours so they don't have to use their weekends for lessons. You can almost make your own schedule in this business, within reason.

WHAT YOU WILL NEED

You may need to have musical instruments to lease to students, but chances are they will either have leased them from a music store, have their own instrument, or be using one provided by their school. If you are teaching larger instruments that are more difficult to move around—such as the piano, harp, or even drums—you will want to have it available in your home for the student to use.

MARKETING ANGLE

One way to market your lessons is to underscore the fact that public education funding is squeezing art and music out of the curriculum. You can fill in the gap for those parents who want to add these cultural elements on their own to give their children a well-rounded education.

NICE TOUCH

Have a group session once a month where all your students can meet each other and commiserate about their lessons, practice, and skill advancement. Create an online newsletter or monitor a chat session with all your students to help them and motivate them in between lessons. Also, always be sure to do a concert once a year. It is important to showcase and celebrate student accomplishment; just make sure it is fun.

EXPANSION POSSIBILITIES

If you start by giving lessons to a couple of individuals, consider offering lessons to groups. Most communities have some space that could be inexpensively rented to hold a class once a week—even the local schools have become more open to community involvement.

You can expand from just children to adults, or vice versa. You can also do consulting work where you help a child decide on an instrument, help them shop for the instrument of their choice, or help beginners upgrade from the instrument they have.

WORDS TO KNOW

Acoustic: An instrument that produces sound by means of physical vibrations; a non-electrified instrument.

Acoustics: The science of sounds.

Perfect pitch: The ability to hear and identify a note without any musical or tonal support.

RESOURCES

Promotion of private music lessons, personalizedmusiclessons.org and musiclessons.tv

JEWELRY MAKING

There are many different ways of getting into the jewelry business and many different types of materials with which you can work. There are also many different types of jewelry to create, from rings to earrings to bracelets to hair clips to pins—and everything in between.

Working in metal will probably require the most in the way of specific tools. You need to be able to heat the metal to manipulate it, and you need metalworking tools to cut and engrave it. But there are many other materials that you can work with to make jewelry—glass, plastic, beads, feathers, even wood, to name just a few.

You need to be quite creative to be a successful jewelry maker. And like everything these days, you need to become familiar with online marketing in order to sell your goods.

HOW THIS BUSINESS IMPACTS YOUR HOME

This business will require a separate studio space with good natural lighting, where you can leave your work-in-progress spread out when you need to leave it for the day,m and have it ready for you to pick up on it when you are ready.

If you find outside outlets to sell your jewelry, you shouldn't need customers coming to your house. If you decide to do a lot of custom work, you probably will want them to be able to come to your studio to look through some gem catalogs or decide what metal they want and to get their finger sized for a ring or measure their wrist for a bracelet.

THINGS TO CONSIDER

The biggest consideration for starting this business is how you are going to sell what you make. If you don't want to do the business end of it and just want to make jewelry, you need to consider hiring a marketing firm or finding a co-op, a retail store, or a web site that will sell your creations.

Another thing to consider, especially if you get into ring making, is that you will probably end up doing some custom work. Someone will like a ring you made but it won't be the right size for them and they will want to know if you will make the ring in their size. You probably should decide ahead of time if custom work is something you want to do. It can be more lucrative but requires a different mindset, including interaction with your customers. And you need to require a deposit for any custom work.

HOW DO YOU WANT TO SPEND YOUR DAY?

This is truly close-up, indoor work. But not only will you be able to get up from your work table and go take a walk with the dog, but you will need to. The best way to avoid physical effects from any type of work—close work, repetitive work, heavy lifting, etc.—is to take regular breaks. Walk around, get outside, look at the landscape instead of the small piece of metal in front of your nose. You will come back refreshed and probably have gained some creative inspiration in the meantime.

WHAT YOU WILL NEED

Jewelry is close work, so you should plan to have magnifying head lamp. What you need for other equipment depends on the kind of material in which you plan to work. Definitely get a large worktable. You may need a board that allows you to pin pieces down while you work on them. You also will need a jeweler's size vice to hold small metal pieces. Working with metal will require a jewelry torch to heat the metal. You will need several different types of pliers—round nose, bent chain nose, and bent chair nose pliers are the three standards. From there you will need jewelry wire, which comes in brass, copper, silver, gold-plated, silver, gold-filled, and silver filled.

The rest depends on what you are making—clasps will be necessary for making bracelets, ear wires for making earrings, etc. You can get prepackaged kits full of all supplies you need depending on what kind of jewelry you plan to make.

MARKETING ANGLE

What kind of jewelry you choose to make will have some bearing on the marketing angle you will need in this business. If you are making beaded bracelets with smiley faces, your marketing approach will be different from what you would use if you decide to make hand-engraved sterling silver rings or gold and diamond pendants.

This is a business where you may need to spend some time setting up tables at craft fairs. You also may want to market your products to jewelry stores and other retail shops, but you need to keep in mind that they buy at a discount, not at full retail. You also have to decide how much time you will have to make enough jewelry to supply retail stores.

NICE TOUCH

Always include care information with your jewelry. Custom and handmade jewelry can be a more expensive purchase than people customarily make. You want to be sure they know how to take care of it. And the nicer it looks, the more people will ask them where they got the piece!

EXPANSION POSSIBILITIES

A great way to expand in this business is to have your own website with selling capabilities. This way, you can reach a broader market and you can sell your products at full retail price.

WORDS TO KNOW

Bezel setting: A type of setting where the stone is placed within a metal seat that surrounds the perimeter of the stone.

Findings: the components—wire, beads, clasps, etc.—contained in a piece of jewelry.

RESOURCES

artbeads.com

jewelrysupply.com

BICYCLE REPAIR 53

They may change color, looks, and handlebar style but bicycles never go out of vogue. For such a constant in everyone's life at one time or another, what couldn't be stable about a business repairing bicycles?

In many parts of the country, this business tends to be seasonal, but you can find ways around that. Rent a storage unit and offer to store people's bicycles over the winter after you do a tuneup and any needed repairs on them. Keep careful track of whose bicycle is whose and you will have work enough to last the entire off season.

If you want to cater to the Lance Armstrong wannabes, you can have business all year round. These roadrace riders are training through snow, sleet, and dark of night and tend to be off the roads only when there is a full-scale blizzard in progress. Some of them work on their own bicycles, but many of them don't, so you can get their business all year. And if you keep Saturday shop hours, you can be sure you will have a group of enthusiasts coming by to talk all things cycling.

HOW THIS BUSINESS IMPACTS YOUR HOME

You can either clear space in the garage or clean out an existing shed and set up shop there. If you have neither, you will at least need to have the room to construct an 8' x 10' or similar sized shed. In the beginning, you can store bicycles in a locking garage and work in the driveway on good days or the porch on bad days, but eventually you will want a work space where you can leave your tools out and store client bicycles while you wait for a part or have time to finish the project.

THINGS TO CONSIDER

Although far from the grease monkey that a car mechanic inevitably becomes during the course of a workday, you still should plan to get greasy working on bicycles. Indulge in coveralls and some rubber gloves to keep your hands and your clothes reasonably clean.

Although there is not a lot of heavy lifting—especially with today's lightweight bicycles—this is close work. And you can spend a lot of the day on your feet.

HOW DO YOU WANT TO SPEND YOUR DAY?

You can get equipment to help take the physical strain out of this job, but you will spend time bent over working with your hands. And you will need to do most of your work under cover, so you will be indoors a good amount of your time.

WHAT YOU WILL NEED

You will need a reasonably clear space to work in with a bench to hold your basic tools—both metric and nonmetric. Purchase a couple of high-quality bicycle stands that allow you to work on the bicycle with it suspended in the air at a height that is comfortable for you. You may want to first get a sense of the types of bicycles you will most commonly be working on before stocking up on too much in the way of supplies, but you should plan to have a small selection of tires and tubes, brake pads, and cables because these are things that need replacement the most.

People typically expect bicycle repair and maintenance work to turn around in a week or so, which gives you time to order most of the parts you need from your regular suppliers.

You will need phone service to take calls for jobs. Plan on a simple computer system to keep track of appointments, do billing, and keep your bookkeeping, as well as to order parts online and search the internet for bicycle-related information. You'll probably want to have a stereo system to keep you entertained while you work.

MARKETING ANGLE

You can choose to direct your efforts toward the more professional-level cyclist or you can stick with the casual rider. The casual rider will probably need your services more than the pro, but they also won't be doing as much work on their bicycle. If you are working on a lot of kids' bikes, market to parents the safety aspect of having a good-working bicycle with adequate brakes and accurate steering.

NICE TOUCH

Always clean any bicycle you work on before giving it back to the owner, even if the work you did was an actual repair and not a spring tune-up. It takes ten minutes to wipe a bicycle down and lubricate the chain. Also, if you see anything simple like a loose screw in a toe clip or something small, tighten it up. Any time you return something in better shape than when it was dropped off, the customer will remember your good service.

Also, make sure there is a space in your driveway/yard designated specifically for your customers. It is frustrating to be a customer and not know where to park, or to be in the way of someone in the household having to leave to get to work. Make sure your customers know you have thought about them.

EXPANSION POSSIBILITIES

You can choose to expand by selling used bicycles and/or helping people narrow down their choices on a new bicycle. Selling new bicycles means having a large inventory that would go way beyond the $5,000 limit of this book and would mean having to have a shop. You could also expand to teaching bicycle safety classes; check into utilizing the local schoolyard on a Saturday morning. You could start early in the spring and do some classes inside to get kids and adults ready for the season.

WORDS TO KNOW

Derailleur: The term for the mechanism that "derails" the chain from one gear to another.

Brake caliper: The clamping mechanism that locks onto the rim of the wheel to stop the bicycle.

Saddle: The technical term for a bicycle seat.

RESOURCES

bikewebsite.com

Bicycling magazine, bicycling.com

Bicycletutor, bicycle repair video tutorials, bicycletutors.com

FENCE INSTALLATIONS 54

Fences are everywhere. They are used to keep things in, to keep things out, and simply for decoration. And they don't last forever, so they need to be repaired and replaced with a certain amount of frequency. Whatever the reason, fence installation work abounds.

The most common fence material is wood. However, vinyl has become a popular fence choice due to its longevity and relative freedom from maintenance. Wrought iron is another common fencing, especially in urban environments. You can have fun shopping for vintage wrought iron fencing at salvage yards.

HOW THIS BUSINESS IMPACTS YOUR HOME

Depending on how busy your fencing business gets, you may need some room in your yard to store fencing until you bring it to the work site. Alternatively, you could have the fencing itself delivered directly from the supplier to the work site. Or you could rent a storage unit to store fencing if it going to be more than a couple days before you install it.

THINGS TO CONSIDER

Although fence installation isn't as back breaking as some construction work, digging holes for fence posts and moving large sections of fencing can be tough. You need to be in good physical shape for this business.

Always protect your body by using a lumbar support belt, wearing sunglasses, and using plenty of sunscreen on exposed skin.

HOW DO YOU WANT TO SPEND YOUR DAY?

If you like to be outside doing physical labor, fencing installation can be rewarding work. While many jobs are mundane, others allow you to use some creativity, such as garden fencing and arbors, and other decorative fencing installations.

WHAT YOU WILL NEED

You will need a high-quality post hole digger, a good shovel, a hand saw as well as power saws (both a skill saw and a table saw), a hacksaw if you work with metal fencing, industrial size shears for vinyl fencing, and a couple of long, heavy-duty extension cords. You should have a weed trimmer to help clear any overgrown areas where fencing will be installed. And you will need a pickup truck or utility van to carry these tools, plus a small trailer for the fencing itself, if you pick it up at the supplier and deliver it to the site.

If your installation includes painting or staining wood fencing, you want to have a supply of industrial quality paint brushes and painting paraphernalia such as paint can openers and clean-up solvents.

Be sure to have a few business signs made to display on site during your work, as well as for a month or so after. Always ask the landowner if this is OK, check at least weekly to see if the sign is still there and in good condition, and be sure to take the sign down after a month or so.

MARKETING ANGLE

If you are doing decorative work, market the "upgrade your home" value of nice fencing. If you are doing fencing installations that are intended to keep kids and pets in the yard, you can market the safety angle. Some fencing installations will be to keep things out of the yard, such as deer—

market the "save your expensive shrubs and trees" angle for these kinds of installations.

NICE TOUCH

Take pictures of your fencing installations; post them on your website or use them on your business card to showcase your work. People love to see their homes used as representative examples of nice work.

EXPANSION POSSIBILITIES

Consider expanding beyond home fencing installations to doing work for businesses. There are always fencing needs for security and to prevent theft of goods and equipment that need to be housed outdoors or in a warehouse.

WORDS TO KNOW

Post hole auger: A power-operated post hole digging tool that screws into the ground, removing dirt as it goes. They are typically operated off the power take off (PTO) on a tractor and should be operated with great caution.

Post hole digger: A hand-operated tool that punches a hole in the ground, and with scissor-like action scoops the dirt out. You do this over and over again until you have reached the desired depth.

PVC: A type of vinyl that has become popular in fencing choice because of its low maintenance.

RESOURCES

betterfences.com

fencguy.com

55 BOAT CLEANING

You should know a little bit about boats to go into this business, but beyond that, you just need to enjoy cleaning things! Boats that are hauled out of the water for the winter or even just for mid-season repairs will need the hull cleaned. And depending on the type of boat, it is a good time to give a major cleaning everything else too—the decks, the sleeping quarters, the head, and the holds. The time to thoroughly clean is when the equipment is not being used.

Where do you find boats to clean? You might start by approaching homes that have a boat sitting in the yard. Marinas that store boats for the winter often will offer a cleaning service in the spring. This either means boats stored at marinas are not potential clients or you could market your services to the marina to contract you to do the boat cleaning they offer their customers.

HOW THIS BUSINESS IMPACTS YOUR HOME

You won't want to drag big boats and park them in your yard to clean them—unless you happen to have a very big yard. This is one of those businesses where you go to the client.

You will need some storage space to house your cleaning equipment and paints and varnishes if you extend your cleaning service to offer paint touch up. But otherwise, this business should not have much impact on your home.

THINGS TO CONSIDER

This is another one of those jobs that revolves around a lot of physical labor. You may be kneeling or bending a lot, trying to squeeze into tight spaces. And you may work with harsh chemicals in order to remove the remnants of the incredible abuse that boats take, especially if they are ocean-going. You should be able to work on most days unless is it pouring rain. If you work with a marina, a lot of the boats you clean may be under cover. But it will be difficult to work in cold winter months since it won't be warm enough to be cleaning decks and having them dry before it freezes.

HOW DO YOU WANT TO SPEND YOUR DAY?

You will be outside doing this work, except for the occasional owner who has a boathouse on their property or if you pursue contract work with marinas (although even many of them do not have undercover storage). And you will be bending and kneeling a lot, and working in tight quarters.

WHAT YOU WILL NEED

You will need appropriate marine cleaning products. You will need to know the difference between the kinds of cleaning products used for fiberglass and wood. You will also need cleaning equipment like mops and brushes, and tools to get dirt out of small crevices.

MARKETING ANGLE

If you are going toward cleaning the high-end boat, you will need to know how to market to wealthy clients. And most of them won't be taking care of hiring the boat cleaning themselves, so know who to market to at the local marinas.

NICE TOUCH

Consider "going green" and using cleansers and other products that are easy on the environment. Promote the greenness of your business to your potential customers.

Also, be sure to point out possible needed repairs while you are working. Sometimes things don't become apparent until they are cleaned.

EXPANSION POSSIBILITIES

You could take your cleaning expertise and get into RV cleaning.

WORDS TO KNOW

Antifouling paint: A durable paint that helps reduce hull cleaning maintenance.

Deck brush: Bristled brush used for cleaning the flat surface of a deck; often found with telescoping handles.

Stain removers: Various products that take stains out of different surfaces, such as fiberglass, metal, or paint.

RESOURCES

boatstoreusa.com

boatersworld.com

RESOURCES

UNITED STATES GOVERNMENT AGENCIES AND BUSINESS ASSOCIATIONS

Small Business Administration (SBA)

6302 Fairview Road, Suite 300

Charlotte, North Carolina 28210

Telephone: 800-827-5722   website: sba.gov

The U.S. Small Business Administration provides new entrepreneurs and existing business owners with financial, technical, and management resources to start, operate and grow a business. To find the local SBA office in your region log onto sba.gov/localresources.index/html.

SBA SERVICES AND PRODUCTS FOR ENTREPRENEURS

U.S. SBA Small Business Start-Up Guide

To order, contact your local SBA to order or log onto sba.gov.

U.S. SBA Business Training Seminars and Courses

For more information, contact your local SBA office or log onto sba.gov/services/training/onlinecourses/index/html.

U.S. SBA Business Plan; Road Map to Success

To order, contact your local SBA office or log onto sba.gov/smallbusinessplanner/plan/writeabusinessplan/index.html.

U.S. SBA Business Financing and Loan Programs

To order loan forms contact your local SBA office or log onto sba.gov/services/financialassistance/sbaloantopics/index.html.

United States Department of Labor:
Office of Small Business Programs (OSBP)
200 Constitution Avenue, NW
Room C-2318
Washington, DC 20210
Telephone: 866-4-USA-DOL   web resource: dol.gov/osbp
OSBP promotes opportunities for small businesses, including small disadvantaged businesses, women-owned small businesses, HUBZone businesses, and businesses owned by service-disabled veterans.

United States Patent and Trademark Office
Commissioners of Patents and Trademarks
(Call or visit USPTO website for specific addresses.)
Telephone: 800-786-9199   website: uspto.gov

United States Copyright Office
Library of Congress
101 Independence Avenue, S.E.
Washington, DC 20559-6000
Public Information Office: 202-707-3000
Forms and publications hotline: 202-707-9100   website: copyright.gov

The Internal Revenue Service (IRS)
Assistance and information for individuals: 800-829-1040
Assistance and information for businesses: 800-829-4933
website: irs.gov
Federal and business tax information from the source.

Service Corps of Retired Executives (SCORE)
409 Third Street, S.W., 6th Floor
Washington, DC 20024
Telephone: 800-634-0245   website: score.org
SCORE is a nonprofit association in partnership with the Small Business Administration to provide aspiring entrepreneurs and business owners with free

business counseling and mentoring programs. The association consists of more than 11,000 volunteer business councilors in 389 regional chapters located throughout the United States. They have helped over 7.2 million small businesses.

U.S. Chamber of Commerce

1615 H Street, N.W.
Washington, DC 20062-2000
Telephone: 202-659-6000
Customer Service: 800-638-6582   website: uschamber.com
The U.S. Chamber of Commerce represents small businesses, corporations, and trade associations from coast to coast. Call 202-659-6000 or log onto their website to locate a regional branch.

United States Association for
Small Businesses and Entrepreneurship

Suite 207, DeSantis Center
Florida Atlantic University-College of Business
777 Glades Road, Boca Raton, FL 33431-0992
Telephone: 561-297-4060   website: usasbe.org
An affiliate of the International Council for Small Business, the USASBE is established to advance knowledge and business education through seminars, conferences, white papers, and various programs.

National Business Incubation Association (NBIA)

20 E. Circle Drive, #37198
Athens, OH 45701-3571
Telephone: 704-593-4331   website: nbia.org
In the United States there are more than 900 business incubation programs, and NBIA provides links to these various incubation programs. Additionally, NBIA assists entrepreneurs with information, education, and networking resources to help in the early development stages of business start-up and the advanced stages of business growth.

National Business Association

P.O. Box 700728

Dallas, Texas 75370

Telephone: 800-456-0440   website: nationalbusiness.org

This nonprofit association assists self-employed individuals and small business owners by using group buying power to provide health plans, educational opportunities and other valuable services.

National Association of Women Business Owners (NAWBO)

8405 Greensboro Drive, Suite #800

McLean, VA 22102

Telephone: 800-55-NAWBO   website: nawbo.org

NAWBO provides women business owner members with support, resources, and business information to help grow and prosper in their own businesses.

UMass Family Business Center

Continuing and Professional Education

100 Venture Way, Suite 201

Hadley, MA 01035

Telephone: 413-545-1537   website: umass.edu/fambiz/

UMass Family Business Center provides members with training programs, information, and workshops to assist with building entrepreneurial skills that can be best utilized in a family-owned and operated business.

National Association for the Self-Employed (NASE)

P.O. Box 612067 DFW Airport

Dallas, TX 75261-2067

Telephone: 800-232-6273   website: nase.org

Founded in 1981, the NASE is an organization whose members include small business owners and professionals who are self-employed. NASE provides members with support, education, and training to help them succeed and prosper in business.

National Small Business Association (NSBA)

1156 15th Street NW, Suite 1100

Washington, D.C. 20005

Telephone: 800-345-6728

website: nsba.biz

A volunteer-based agency focusing on small business advocacy in an effort to promote federal policies of benefit to small businesses and the growth of free enterprise. Since 1937, the NSBA has grown from representing 160 small businesses to representing over 150,000.

International Franchise Association (IFA)

1501 K Street, N.W., Suite 350

Washington, D.C. 20005

Telephone: 202-628-8000

website: franchise.org

IFA membership organization includes franchisers, franchisees, and service and product suppliers for the franchising industry.

BUSINESS BOOKS AND PUBLICATIONS

Suggested Reading

The 30 Second Commute: The Ultimate Guide to Starting and Operating a Home-Based Business, Beverley Williams and Don Cooper, New York: McGraw-Hill, 2004

101+ Answers to the Most Frequently Asked Questions From Entrepreneurs, Courtney H. Price, New York: John Wiley & Sons, 1999.

303 Marketing Tips: Guaranteed to Boost Your Business!, Rieva Lesonsky and Leann Anderson, Irvine, CA: Entrepreneur Press, 1999.

Ben Franklin's 12 Rules of Management: The Founding Father of American Business Solves Your Toughest Business Problems, Blaine McCormick, Irvine, CA: Entrepreneur Press, 2000.

The Best Home Businesses for the 21st Century: The Inside Information You Need to Know to Select a Home-Based Business That's Right for You, Paul and Sarah Edwards, Los Angeles, CA: J.P Tarcher, 1999.

The Book of Entrepreneurs' Wisdom: Classic Writings by Legendary Entrepreneurs,
Peter Krass, New York: John Wiley & Sons, 1999

Business Plans Made Easy: It's Not as Hard as You Think!, Mark Henricks, Irvine,
CA: Entrepreneur Press, 1999.

The Complete Idiot's Guide to Starting a Home-Based Business, Second Edition,
Barbara Weltman and Beverly Williams, Indianapolis, IL: Alpha Books, 2000.

The Customer Revolution, Patricia B. Seybold, New York: Crown Publishing, 2001.

*E-Service: 24 Ways to Keep Your Customers When the Competition is Just a Click
Away*, Ron Zemke and Thomas K. Connellan, New York: AMACOM, 2000.

The Entrepreneur Next Door, Bill Wagner, Irvine, CA: Entrepreneur Press, 2006.

*The Entrepreneur's Internet Handbook: Your Legal and Practical Guide to Starting a
Business Website*, Hugo Barreca and Julia K. O'Neill, Naperville, IL:
Sourcebooks, 2002.

Entrepreneur's Toolkit: Tools and Techniques to Launch and Grow Your New Business
(Harvard Business Essentials), Richard Luecke, Harvard Business School
Press, 2004.

*The Girl's Guide to Starting Your Own Business : Candid Advice, Frank Talk, and True
Stories for the Successful Entrepreneur*, Caitlin Friedman and Kimberly Yorio,
Collins, 2004.

Grow Your Business, Mark Henricks, Irvine, CA: Entrepreneur Press, 2001.

Homebased Business Tax Deductions, Stephen Fishman and Diana Fitzpatrick,
Berkeley, CA: Nolo Press, 2007.

How To Dotcom: A Step-by-Step Guide to e-Commerce, Robert McGarvey, Irvine,
CA: Entrepreneur Press, 2000.

How to Sell Collectibles on eBay, Entrepreneur Press and Jennifer A. Ericcson,
Irvine, CA: Entrepreneur Press, Third Edition, 2006.

If at First You Don't Succeed... : The Eight Patterns of Highly Effective Entrepreneurs,
Brent Bowers, New York: Currency, 2006

Import/Export: How to Get Started in International Trade, Carl A. Nelson, New
York: McGraw-Hill, 2000.

Knock Out Marketing: Powerful Strategies to Punch Up Your Sales, Jack Ferreri,
Irvine, CA: Entrepreneur Press, 1999.

Legal Guide For Starting & Running A Small Business (8th Edition), Fred S. Steingold and Ilona M. Bray, Berkeley, CA: NOLO, 2005

Masters of Success, Ivan R. Misner and Don Morgan, Irvine, CA: Entrepreneur Press, 2005

Permission Based E-Mail Marketing That Works!, Kim MacPherson and Rosalind Resnick, Chicago: Dearborn Trade, 2001.

Positioning: The Battle for Your Mind, Al Ries and Jack Trout, New York: McGraw-Hill, 2001.

Public Relations Kit for Dummies, Eric Yaverbaum and Bill Bly, Foster City, CA: Hungry Minds Inc., 2001.

Quick Guide to Working at Home, Hugh Williams, London: Lawpack, 2008.

Six-Week Start-Up: A Step-By-Step Program for Starting Your Business, Making Money, and Achieving Your Goals!, Rhonda Abrams, Palo Alto, CA: Planning Shop 2004.

Spare Room Startup: How to Start a Business from Home, Emma Jones, Petersfield, Hampshire, UK: Harriman House, 2008.

Start Your Own Business, Rieva Lesonsky, Irvine, CA: Entrepreneur Press, 2001.

Start Your Own Business: The Only Start-Up Book You'll Ever Need, Rieva Lesonsky, Irvine, CA: Entrepreneur Press, Third Edition, 2004.

Start Your Own Senior Services Business, Jacquelyn Lynn and Charlene Davis, Irvine, CA: Entrepreneur Press, 2006.

Start Your Real Estate Career, Rich Mintzer, Irvine, CA: Entrepreneur Press, 2006

Starting on a Shoestring: Building a Business Without a Bankroll, Arnold S. Goldstein, New York: John Wiley & Sons, 2002

Straight Talk About Starting and Growing Your Business, Sanjyot P. Dunung, New York, McGraw-Hill, 2005

Successful Business Planning in 30 Days: A Step-By-Step Guide for Writing a Business Plan and Starting Your Own Business, Third Edition, Peter J. Patsula, Petsula Media, 2004

Think Big: Nine Ways to Make Millions From Your Ideas, Don Debelak, Irvine, CA: Entrepreneur Press, 2001.

Time Tested Advertising Methods, John Caples and Fred E. Hahn, Upper Saddle River, NJ: Prentice Hall, 1998.

The Way to the Top: The Best Business Advice I Ever Received, Donald Trump, New York: Crown Business, 2004

Unofficial Guide to Starting a Business Online, Jason R. Rich, New York: John Wiley & Sons, 2006

The Unofficial Guide to Starting a Small Business, Marcia Layton Turner, New York: John Wiley & Sons, 2004

Where's the Money? Sure-Fire Financing Solutions for Your Small Business, Art Beroff and Dwayne Moyers, Irvine, CA: Entrepreneur Media Inc., 1999.

Work at Home Directory, Barbara Becker, Prime Publishing, 2007.

MAGAZINES

e-Business Advisor, Advisor Media Inc. P.O. Box 429002, San Diego, CA 92142-9002. 858-278-5600 advisor.com

Business Week, The McGraw-Hill Companies. P.O. Box 182604, Columbus, OH 43272. 877-833-5524 businessweek.com

Entrepreneur, Entrepreneur Media Inc. 2445 McCabe Way, Irvine, CA 92614. 800-274-6229 entrepreneur.com

Family Business, Family Business Publishing Company. 1845 Walnut Street, Suite 900, Philadelphia, PA 19103. 800-637-4464 familybusinessmagazine.com

Fast Company, Forbes. 90 5th Avenue, New York, NY 10011. 800-295-0893 forbes.com

Franchise Times. 2808 Anthony Lane , S. Mpls, MN 55418. 800-528-3296 franchisetimes.com

Home Business, homebusinessmag.com

Inc. 100 First Avenue, 4th Floor, Building 36, Charlestown, MA 02129. 800-234-0999 inc.com

Marketers Forum, Forum Publishing Company. 383 E. Main Street, Centerport, NY 11721. 800-635-7654 forum123.com

Opportunity World and Money 'N Profits, United Communication. 130 Church St. #257 NY, NY 10007. 212-786-0291 oppworld.com

Promo. P.O. Box 10587, Riverton, NJ 08076-8575. 800-775-3777 promomagazine.com

SMALL BUSINESS SOFTWARE

Business Plan Pro
Palo Alto Software

The Standard version comes with more than 500 business plans to learn from and more than 9,000 industry profiles, while the Premier version adds collaboration tools and business valuation analysis. Both are designed to help launch entrepreneurs on their way to tremendous success.

Business Plan Pro: eBay Edition
Palo Alto Software

As eBay has grown into a unique home for thousands of businesses, the need for specialized business plans has emerged. This special addition includes eBay specific example, sales forecasts and more.

Marketing Plan Pro
Palo Alto Software

From the initial budget breakdown and spreadsheets to the final marketing plan, this software has the necessary tools for implementing a marketing strategy and putting together a top-notch plan for any size business.

Microsoft Office Small Business Accounting
Microsoft

Designed for Windows XP, Small Business Accounting helps the owner, manager or bookkeeper handle all financial matters from tracking inventory and payroll to putting together all necessary financial reports.

Microsoft Office Small Business Management Edition 2006

Microsoft

Also designed for Windows XP, Business Management helps business owners and managers keep track of sales information, cash flow, invoices and the numerous details of running a company.

QuickBooks Pro 2006

Intuit, Inc.

Mac & PC versions offer a wide range of financial and accounting options which include allow you to track sales and expenses, pay bills, handle payroll, track inventory and create estimates and reports for small or homebased businesses. The programs are designed to easily interface with many PC or Mac programs as necessary.

Quicken Premier Home & Business 2006

Intuit, Inc.

Easy-to-navigate financial software for home and small businesses as well as self-employed professionals. This PC-based program is designed to handle all common business billing and tax basics while helping you monitor expenses and keep tabs on assets. The Mac version is also very popular and helps small business professionals manage cash, pay bills, and handle additional financial details.

INTERNET AND E-COMMERCE RESOURCES

All Business

allbusiness.com

You'll find numerous articles and plenty of tips and information in the Advice Center at this very comprehensive web business center. You can also search articles from 700 business periodicals, download business forms or check out numerous business guides and directories.

Bplans

Bplans.com

Expert advice, business planning tools, and many sample business plans for numerous types of businesses are available from Bplans.com. Articles, expert advices, resources, and software are all part of this comprehensive site.

Entrepreneur Online

entrepreneur.com

This is your one-stop source for small business information, products, and services online. View current articles from Entrepreneur magazine, get expert advice for all your small business questions, and browse through the thousands of small business and franchise opportunities featured on the site. It's all here in one convenient location and has been specifically developed to help entrepreneurs start, run, and grow their small businesses.

Cafepress.com

cafepress.com

Cafepress lets you build a store for your website that features promotional products such as T-shirts and hats with your company logo or message emblazoned on them. They are unique in that they create your products at their site and ship the products directly to your online customers. No costly inventory to purchase. Cafepress does it all for you and you keep a portion of the profits from every sale.

CNNMoney

cnnmoney.com

The markets, business news, and plenty of articles on personal finance, real estate and, of course, small business highlight this major site from CNN, designed to keep readers on top of the latest financial news. The Small Business section includes articles, newsletters, podcasts, and calculators. The latest in small business news is updated regularly to help you on top of the currency industry trends and economic factors.

MerchantExpress.com

merchantexpress.com

Merchant Express provides internet entrepreneurs, homebased business owners, and retail storefront owners merchant accounts and credit card processing options and solutions. Increase revenues and improve customer services by providing your customers with credit card payment options.

My Own Business

myownbusiness.org

An online course on starting a business originally developed after the California riots in 1992 as a bricks-and-mortar business to teach young people about going into business. A free14-session course is offered, plus an $85 certified course and textbook. The site also offers a range of resources, business term glossary and more.

Nolo.com

nolo.com

Nolo.com is the one-stop source for online law information and legal forms pertaining to small business, employees, trademarks, and copyrights. If it has to do with the law, you will find it here. This site is large, easy to navigate, and jam-packed full of legal advice, books, forms, software and information.

Startup Journal

startupjournal.com

The Wall Street Journal Center for Entrepreneurs includes leading columnists, plus articles on financing, e-commerce and various new business ideas. You can also find businesses and franchises for sale and various business opportunities plus a well-stocked business bookstore and much more.

INDEX